Ukraine

Ukraine: Contested Nationhood in a European Context challenges the common view that Ukraine is a country split between a pro-European West and a pro-Russian East. The volume navigates the complicated cultural history of Ukraine and highlights the importance of regional traditions for an understanding of the current political situation. A key feature is the different politics of memory that prevail in each region, such as the Soviet past being presented as either a foreign occupation or a benign socialist project.

The pluralistic culture of Ukraine (in terms of languages, national legacies and religions) forms a nation that faces both internal and external challenges. In order to address this fully, rather than following a merely chronological order, this book examines different interpretations of Ukrainian nationhood that have been especially influential, such as the Russian tradition, the Habsburg past and the Polish connections.

Finally, the book analyses Ukraine's political and economic options for the future. Can the desired integration into EU structures overcome the concentration of investment of power in the hands of a few oligarchs and a continuing widespread culture of corruption? Will proposals to join NATO, which garnered robust support among the populace in the aftermath of the Russian aggression, materialise under the current circumstances? Is the political culture in Ukraine sufficiently functional to guarantee democratic procedures and the rule of law?

Ulrich Schmid is Professor of Russian Studies at the University of St Gallen, Switzerland. His research interests include nationalism, popular culture and media in Eastern Europe. He studied German and Slavic literature at the Universities of Zürich, Heidelberg, and Leningrad. He has held academic positions in Basel, Bern, Bochum, and was a visiting researcher at Harvard University, in Warsaw, and in Oslo. His publications include *Regionalism without Regions: Reconceptualizing Ukraine's Heterogeneity* (ed. 2019); *De Profundis: On the Failure of the Russian Revolution* (ed. 2017); *Technologies of the Soul: The Production of Truth in Contemporary Russian Culture* (2015); *Sword, Eagle and Cross: The Aesthetics of the Nationalist Discourse in Interwar Poland* (ed. 2013) and *Tolstoi as a Theological Thinker and Critic of the Church* (ed. 2013).

Europa Country Perspectives

The *Europa Country Perspectives* series, from Routledge, examines a wide range of contemporary political, economic, developmental and social issues from areas around the world. Complementing the *Europa Regional Surveys of the World series, Europa Country Perspectives* is a valuable resource for academics, students, researchers, policymakers, business people and anyone with an interest in current world affairs.

While the *Europa World Year Book* and its associated Regional Surveys inform on and analyse contemporary economic, political and social developments at the national and regional level, Country Perspectives provide in-depth, country-specific volumes written or edited by specialists in their field, delving into a country's particular situation. Volumes in the series are not constrained by any particular template, but may explore a country's recent political, economic, international relations, social, defence, or other issues in order to increase understanding.

Greece in the 21st Century: The Politics and Economics of a Crisis
Edited by Constantine Dimoulas and Vassilis K. Fouskas

The Basque Contention: Ethnicity, Politics, Violence
Ludger Mees

Bolivia: Geopolitics of a Landlocked State
Ronald Bruce St John

The Taiwan Issue: Problems and Prospects
Benjamin Schreer and Andrew T. H. Tan

Ukraine: Contested Nationhood in a European Context
Ulrich Schmid

For more information about this series, please visit: www.routledge.com/Europa-Country-Perspectives/book-series/ECP

Ukraine
Contested Nationhood in a European Context

Ulrich Schmid

**Translated by
Roy Sellars**

LONDON AND NEW YORK

First published 2020
by Routledge
2 Park Square, Milton Park, Abingdon, Oxon OX14 4RN

and by Routledge
711 Third Avenue, New York, NY 10017

Routledge is an imprint of the Taylor & Francis Group, an informa business

First issued in paperback 2021

© 2020 Ulrich Schmid

The right of Ulrich Schmid to be identified as author of this work has been asserted by him in accordance with sections 77 and 78 of the Copyright, Designs and Patents Act 1988.

All rights reserved. No part of this book may be reprinted or reproduced or utilised in any form or by any electronic, mechanical, or other means, now known or hereafter invented, including photocopying and recording, or in any information storage or retrieval system, without permission in writing from the publishers.

Trademark notice: Product or corporate names may be trademarks or registered trademarks, and are used only for identification and explanation without intent to infringe.

Based on a text originally published in Switzerland as:

Ukraine zwischen Ost und West, by Ulrich Schmid

© Ulrich Schmid, 2015, Vontobel-Stiftung

Europa Regional Editor, Eastern Europe, Russia and Central Asia: Dominic Heaney

Editorial Assistant: Lucy Pritchard

British Library Cataloguing-in-Publication Data
A catalogue record for this book is available from the British Library

Library of Congress Cataloging-in-Publication Data
A catalog record has been requested for this book

ISBN: 978-0-367-19980-7 (hbk)
ISBN: 978-1-03-208595-1 (pbk)
ISBN: 978-0-429-24450-6 (ebk)

Typeset in Times New Roman
by Taylor & Francis Books

Contents

	List of figures	vi
1	Where is Ukraine?	1
2	How many Ukraines are there? Seeing the East-West opposition in context	8
3	The Russian perspective: 'Little Russia' in the 'Russian World'	18
4	The cultivation of the Habsburg myth in Galicia and Bukovina	32
5	Poland as friend and foe: From the Volhynia Massacre to the Polish initiatives for Ukraine in the EU	41
6	National independence and regional differences	49
7	History wars over the tragedies of the Soviet era	57
8	The Ukraine crisis: Civil war or Russian hybrid war?	68
9	The Ukrainian economy	77
10	The European Union as unwilling protector of Ukraine	85
11	The complicated relationship with the USA and NATO	93
12	*Quo vadis*, Ukraine?	99
	Appendix	104
	Bibliography	112
	Index	113

Figures

1.1	Ukraine in the inter-war years	3
2.1	Do you agree that all inhabitants of Ukraine should master the Ukrainian language?	10
2.2	Do you agree that all inhabitants of Ukraine should master the Russian language?	11
4.1	Ukraine in the nineteenth century	33
6.1	The regions of Ukraine	49
10.1	Support for EU integration	89
10.2	Do you feel European?	90
11.1	Support for Ukraine joining NATO	97

1 Where is Ukraine?

In September 2014, I boarded a bus in Košice, the 2013 European Capital of Culture, in eastern Slovakia, and travelled to Uzhhorod, the border town in Ukraine. The distance was 100 kilometres, the fare 7 Euros, and the journey time three and a half hours – including a meticulous border control check, lasting nearly an hour. The driver's transactions of his personal business also lasted a considerable time; he mostly delivered paint and varnish at various stops during the journey, thereby supplementing his not particularly attractive wage.

The last village in the European Union, at the border between Slovakia and Ukraine, is called Vyšné Nemecké – its original name, fittingly, was 'Oberdeutschdorf'. A border post is located there, that, with its military fortifications, recalls Soviet crossing points. The behaviour of the mostly Ukrainian bus passengers also was still determined by Soviet norms. The bus had only just driven into the customs area when a reverential silence set in. The women and men now spoke to each other only in whispers, the bus driver turned off the Slovakian pop radio station and the homogenised American English warbling fell silent. A wondrous change was also noticeable in the driver's choice of language: while in Košice, he had barked in Russian at passengers boarding his bus that they should stow their luggage in the hold, he now spoke in correct Ukrainian with the border officials as he collected the passengers' passports. The bus stood in the customs clearance hall for a long time, until finally all the documents had been checked and stamped. We were lucky: on our bus, there were no young Russian men of an age fit for military service. For these young men, entry into Ukraine had been banned since Spring 2014. A change in the ambience also made itself felt; the driver now tuned into a Ukrainian channel that broadcast mostly Russian hits, so-called *Popsa*.

From the 'German Heights' the road goes directly down to Uzhhorod, which already belongs to the expanded Europe of the 47 member states of the Council of Europe. Just how haphazard and ephemeral the attachment to a nation state can be is clearly evident from the eventful history of this region. Until the First World War, Uzhhorod was called Ungvár and belonged to the Hungarian half of the dual monarchy forming the Habsburg Empire. In 1910,

2 Where is Ukraine?

80 per cent of the town's inhabitants were Hungarian and barely 4 per cent were Ukrainian. The region soon fell into the grinder of the twentieth century. Following the Paris peace treaties, Uzhhorod and the attached Transcarpathia were ascribed to newly independent Czechoslovakia. The authorities did their best to turn Uzhhorod into a Czechoslovak city and built a new administrative district. Many of these buildings were erected under the influence of the so-called 'Rondocubism' which was meant to become the national architectural style of the young state. In the Second World War, the Red Army occupied this territory. Stalin then incorporated Transcarpathia into the Ukrainian Soviet Republic. Ultimately Uzhhorod became, in 1991, the westernmost regional capital of an independent Ukraine. The town's population ratio has been precisely inverted by comparison with 1910: today 77 per cent of the inhabitants of Uzhhorod are Ukrainian while barely 7 per cent are Hungarian.[1] Nostalgia for the dual monarchy and for Czechoslovakia is still present, though. On the riverbank promenade in Uzhhorod, a small memorial is found for the Good Soldier Švejk, with a melancholy quotation from Jaroslav Hašek's eponymous novel: 'And thus was our Franz Ferdinand slain.'[2]

Various cultures, languages, nations and states meet and clash in this contact zone. Its eventful history has left lasting traces on the political map as well. Near Uzhhorod there is virtually an intersection of four countries: here the borders of Poland, Slovakia, Hungary and Ukraine are barely 50 kilometres away from one another. And it should not be forgotten that Poland and Romania had a common border in the inter-war years (Figure 1.1), running between Kolomyia, the town in eastern Galicia, and Cernăuți (Chernivtsi), the formerly Austrian town of Czernowitz that was occupied by Romania after the First World War. In this region the cultural dynamics of European national history are quite tangible.

The European relevance of Transcarpathia can also be seen in the fact that one of the midpoints of Europe is located in this region. Varying according to the method of calculation and the geographical definition, the midpoint may lie in Lithuania, Bavaria, the Czech Republic, Slovakia – or in this Transcarpathian region of Ukraine. In 1887, a memorial stone was erected in Rakhiv indicating the geodetic centre of Europe.

What holds for Transcarpathia on a local level is also true, *mutatis mutandis*, for the whole of Ukraine. In 1995, the US historian Mark von Hagen published an important essay with the provocative title 'Does Ukraine Have a History?'[3] He maintains that the flexibility of its borders, the permeability of its cultures and its multi-ethnic society make Ukrainian history a highly modern field of investigation that poses a challenge to the conceptual dominance of the nation state in historiography.

Precisely because of its complicated history, Ukraine only became an object of academic research quite recently. The past of the individual Ukrainian regions used to be treated, at best, in the framework of Russian, Polish, Czechoslovak, Romanian, Austrian or Hungarian national history. A notable exception here is Mykhailo Hrushevsky's *History of the Ukraine-Rus'* in ten

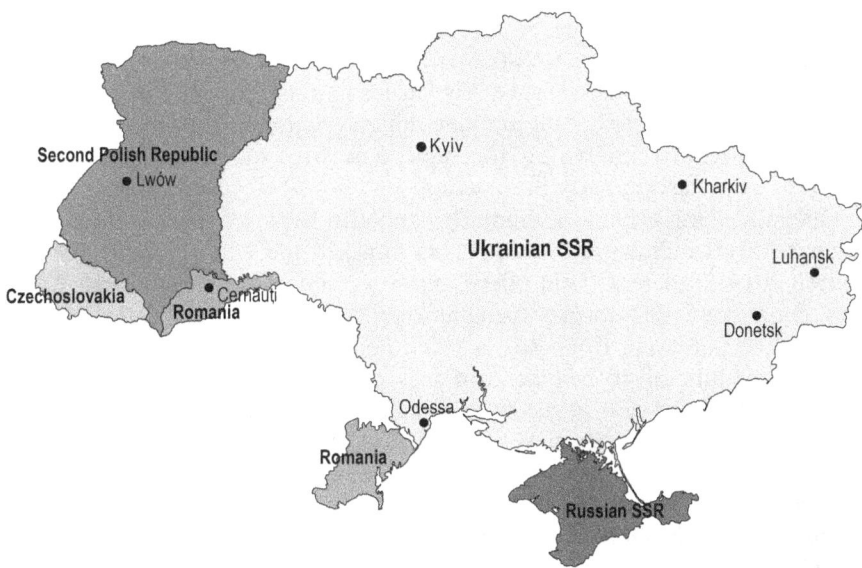

Figure 1.1 Ukraine in the inter-war years

volumes (1895–1933).[4] Not until the late 1980s did Ukraine attract any attention from historians. This also has very much to do with a paradigm change in historiography: the French *Annales* School turned away from the classical history of events and investigated the emergence of values, mentalities and life worlds in a broader cultural context. In Germany, the history of ideas became established in the 1970s, devoted to researching the perception of social realities. Around the same time Hayden White published his influential book *Metahistory*,[5] thereby initiating a new trend that has by now become dominant in historiography. Most historians today are no longer concerned with historical events in themselves but rather with their representations in public discourse and collective memory.

Set against the backdrop of the transformed research interests found in the academic study of history, Ukraine no longer appears the exception but rather the rule. Here there are no 'great men' such as Napoleon, Bismarck or Stalin who, with their political biographies, seem to dominate the history of entire epochs. In Ukraine, down to the present day, quite different traditions come together that have mutually influenced each other. Understanding Ukraine thus always means taking into account the various threads of culture that attract each other, repulse each other and at key historical moments also interlace.

The dramatic events of 2014 made clear how explosive this mixture of differing historical narratives can be. Diametrically opposed interpretations of reality collided and are still colliding. The Kremlin maintains that a civil war is going on in Ukraine; after the fall of President Yanukovych, a 'fascist junta' supposedly seized power in Kyiv (Kiev), and in Donetsk and Luhansk, a 'people's militia' was formed that is defending itself against the oppression of the new dictatorship. Conversely, according to this interpretation, the regime in Kyiv is carrying out punitive military action against its own citizens in the east of the country. At the same time Moscow insists that it is not involved as a warring party in the conflict.

Officially Russia holds a similarly stubborn view in the Crimean crisis. After a covert military invasion, Russia annexed the Ukrainian peninsula in March 2014. President Putin talked about a 'reunion' of Crimea with Russia and maintained that former General Secretary Khrushchev had arbitrarily severed the peninsula from Russia when he awarded it to Ukraine in 1954. The referendum of 16 March 2014 was thus lawful and, with the alleged approval of 96 per cent of the population of Crimea, it prepared the way for joining the Russian Federation.

From the Kyiv perspective, events present themselves quite differently: Russia annexed Crimea in contravention of international law, and not only incited the war in Donbas but also orchestrated it militarily. The Ukrainian army's course of action against the separatists in Donbas was consequently designated as an 'Anti-Terrorist Operation' (ATO). In view of the impossibility of a military solution, this strategy was officially abandoned in April 2018 and replaced by a 'Joint Forces Operation'. Kyiv also refuses to negotiate directly with the leaders of the 'People's Republics' of Donetsk and Luhansk, and accuses Moscow of waging an undeclared war against Ukraine.

However, the lines of conflict do not always run as clearly as they do in the most recent confrontations. The cultural history of Ukraine is rich in discussions of both self-images and images as perceived by others, discussions of relations to other ethnic minorities, and discussions of the imperialism of foreign powers.

In the early twenty-first century, the central question that arises in all urgency is this: can Ukraine preserve its unity as a state? The answer turns out to be either positive or negative, according to which model of interpretation is applied to the complexities of Ukrainian culture. Roughly speaking, it is possible to identify two different approaches. First, following Samuel P. Huntington,[6] different cultural spaces may be identified in Ukraine. The dividing line would run right through the middle of the present state territory, clearly dividing Western civilisation from Orthodox civilisation. The logical consequence of this interpretation would be a demand for Ukraine to be split up, a process which would ideally be carried out following the model of Czechoslovakia in 1993.

The second approach does not emphasise rootedness in a certain cultural tradition but instead the formation of a European system of values in the whole of Ukraine. In this view, the unity of Ukraine is not founded in terms of culture or even ethnicity, but rather by means of the consensus of citizens in a civil society.

In the 1990s, Russia and Ukraine developed in a largely parallel way: the socialist economic system was replaced by a predatory capitalism in which a small and privileged elite quickly took shape, while the broader population lived close to the poverty line. In 2000, however, the two states parted ways. In Russia, President Putin set up a vertical axis of power and thus transitioned to a 'managed democracy'. The boom years up until the financial crisis of 2008 brought fabulous growth figures for the Russian economy, and approval ratings for President Putin were correspondingly high.

In Ukraine, a similar scenario – which would certainly have served to preserve the interests of the Ukrainian power elite – failed, and the so-called Gongadze affair, in 2000, marked the turning point. Georgiy Gongadze (1969–2000) was a journalist, critical of the regime, who was murdered in unexplained circumstances. Not long after, tape recordings came to light which heavily incriminated the president at the time, Leonid Kuchma (born in 1938). The so-called 'cassette scandal' led to the emergence of a critical awareness in the Ukrainian public. The events of the Orange Revolution in 2004 showed even more clearly how high the readiness for political engagement had become. After Viktor Yanukovych (born in 1950) had declared himself the winner in a rigged presidential election, over 100,000 people took to the streets in Kyiv to protest against the electoral fraud. Although the demonstrators achieved their goal, in that the run-off election was repeated and Viktor Yushchenko (born in 1954) took over the presidency until 2010. In retrospect, the years of the 'Orange' government must, however, be counted as lost time. The former allies Viktor Yushchenko and Yulia Tymoshenko (born in 1960) squandered a lot of energy in bouts of infighting and soon fought with each other almost to the point of bloodshed. The sad result of this internal power struggle was the legally correct selection of the vote-rigger of 2004 as President of Ukraine in 2010. Viktor Yanukovych attempted to install a regime in Ukraine that would be just as authoritarian as in Russia. One case in point was that of the so-called *Titushki*. On 18 May 2013, a 'Rise Ukraine' rally in Kyiv was attacked by thugs. One of the most wicked hooligans was Vadym Titushko, who beat up two journalists. He involuntarily rose to dubious fame, and his name became synonymous with paid hooligans in Yanukovych's service who would attack demonstrations by the political opposition. Initially, the daily rate was about $20 but with the growing intensity of the Euromaidan demonstrations in Independence Square, the price quickly rose to $100.[7]

However, the development of Ukrainian civil society had already reached a high enough level so that a Russian scenario was no longer possible. After Yanukovych refused in November 2013 to put his signature to an EU Association Agreement that had been negotiated in detail, the Euromaidan protests began in Kyiv. For weeks on end, with temperatures below freezing, a great mass of people gathered together on Kyiv's Independence Square, advocating a better future for the country. The demonstrations in favour of EU integration soon transformed into protests against the corrupt and nepotistic regime of President Yanukovych; and the demonstrations met an abrupt end when, on 20 February 2014, snipers fired into the crowd.

However tragic the events at the Euromaidan may have been, they also prove that the formation of a democratic and constitutional awareness in Ukraine is irreversible. Above all, the post-Soviet generation no longer defines itself in ethnic categories but rather in terms of citizenship. Thus, 89 per cent of young people in Donetsk describe themselves as 'citizens of Ukraine', whereas around 30 per cent of older people still perceive of themselves as 'Soviet'.[8]

Proposals to divide Ukraine up according to a Czechoslovak model fail to take account of the complex situation of values, cultures, languages and confessions in Ukraine. There is no predetermined point for a division. In Czechoslovakia, a Czech constituent republic and a Slovak constituent republic had already been created in 1968 by the federalisation of the state. How should Ukraine be divided, though – at the former eastern border of the Second Polish Republic, or at the River Dnieper, which divides Ukraine into two halves of roughly equivalent size? What would happen to the centre of the country, which admittedly has a long Soviet and Russian past, but has also formed its own political values and standpoints in the meantime?

It is difficult to predict how the Ukraine crisis will end. It can be assumed with some certainty, though, that the answer to this question will be given not in Kyiv but in Moscow. President Putin began a very great game in 2014, in which he has himself become a prisoner now; on it Putin has staked the international reputation of Russia as a reliable partner and energy supplier. The flight of capital out of Russia has taken on previously unknown dimensions, and the climate for foreign direct investments has become very unfavourable. The economic malaise has been aggravated at least temporarily by the falling price of crude oil and the crisis of the rouble.

On the other hand, Putin has managed by means of his aggressive Ukraine policy to close ranks behind him in terms of domestic politics. The trauma of the street protests in the run-up to the presidential elections of 2012 has been overcome. Since the annexation of Crimea, Putin has consistently been achieving approval ratings of over 80 per cent. Furthermore, he has trumped the opposition – in which there are several proponents of nationalism – by playing the patriotic card. Even the blogger Alexei Navalny (born in 1976), one of Putin's harshest critics, expressed the opinion in a radio interview in October 2014 that he would not give Crimea back to Ukraine if he were the President of Russia.

As long as Putin remains in power, which may last until 2024, it is not possible to count on a long-term peaceful solution for Donbas. A destabilised Eastern Ukraine delivers just what Moscow wants; the 'People's Republics' of Donetsk and Luhansk stick like a thorn in the flesh of Ukraine, so that it is prevented from any further integration with the West.

The precarious situation in Ukraine will not be able to change until the Russian public protests against Putin's policy line, a line which is as risky as it is cynical; at the moment such a scenario appears rather unlikely. For one thing, the Russian propaganda machine works highly efficiently and draws a black-and-white picture of what is going on in Ukraine; and, second, immediately after his election into his third term as president, Putin touchily limited the right to demonstrate. Those participating in unapproved protest meetings are threatened with heavy fines and even, in cases of assault on the forces of law and order, with prison sentences. Whoever takes to the streets in Russia needs a lot of courage.

Notes

1 Károly Kocsis and Eszter Kocsisné Hódosi, *Hungarian Minorities in the Carpathian Basin: A Study in Ethnic Geography* (Toronto, 1995), p. 49.
2 See Jaroslav Hašek, *The Good Soldier Švejk*, trans. Cecil Parrott (London, 2016).
3 Mark von Hagen, 'Does Ukraine Have a History?', *Slavic Review*, LIV/3 (1995), pp. 658–673.
4 See Mykhailo Hrushevsky, *History of the Ukraine-Rus'*, vol. I, trans. Marta Skorupsky, ed. Andrzej Poppe and Frank E. Sysyn (Edmonton, 1997).
5 Hayden White, *Metahistory: The Historical Imagination in Nineteenth-century Europe* (Baltimore, MD, 1973).
6 See Samuel P. Huntington, *The Clash of Civilizations and the Remaking of World Order* (New York, 1996).
7 Andrew Wilson, *Ukraine Crisis: What It Means for the West* (New Haven, CT, 2014), p. 78.
8 Yaroslav Hrytsak, 'On the Relevance and Irrelevance of Nationalism in Contemporary Ukraine', in *A Laboratory of Transnational History: Ukraine and Recent Ukrainian Historiography*, ed. Georgiy Kasianov and Philipp Ther (Budapest, 2009), pp. 225–248, p. 232.

2 How many Ukraines are there?
Seeing the East-West opposition in context

The Ukrainian writer and publicist Mykola Riabchuk published an essay in 1992 in which he took the cultural heterogeneity of Ukraine as his theme and spoke of 'two Ukraines', such that the European West was confronted by an East with Soviet characteristics.[1] In Galicia, with its capital Lviv (Lwów, Lvov, Lemberg), there was a Ukrainian national awareness that could draw upon a Greek Catholic cultural tradition, while Donbas, with its centre Donetsk (Yuzovka from 1869–1924, Stalin from 1924–1929, Stalino from 1929–1961), had defined itself as a Russian and later as a Soviet province. The West showed evidence of an autonomous identity, while in the East a 'creolisation' of Russian and Ukrainian traditions could be observed. The differences were great in social terms as well, according to Riabchuk. The West, because it belonged first to the Austrian monarchy and later to the Second Polish Republic, had a bourgeois tradition at its disposal; the East, on the other hand, was rooted in peasant and proletarian structures.

Riabchuk emphasised, though, that these 'two Ukraines' did not exist 'next to each other' but rather 'in one another'. At each 'pole of the Ukrainian globe' a particular possibility of development was set up: the 'return to Europe' or 'immersing in Eurasia', the 'attainment of an independent Ukrainian identity' or 'definitively dissolving in the Soviet, the Orthodox and the East Slavic'.

Riabchuk later supplemented his conception with a further aspect. Proceeding from the conclusion that there was no clear demarcation line between Western and Eastern Ukraine, he spoke of a 'third Ukraine' which was 'unarticulated, undefined, undefinable and ambivalent'; and he did not simply stop at this assessment either. For Riabchuk's analysis in terms of cultural studies turned out to entail a quasi-medical diagnosis: the cultural heterogeneity of Ukraine was thus 'ambivalent and split', and Ukrainians' 'neurosis' and 'traumas' would be further heightened by the external pressure coming from Russia.

Riabchuk's arguments were widely discussed in the run-up to the Orange Revolution of 2004. His conception is based on the normative idea that a nation state ought to have a unitary language and culture at its disposal. Riabchuk thus leaves out the fact that, first, the ethnically homogeneous nation state by no means represents a rule without exceptions in Europe, and, second, nation states have always only arisen as the result of cultural homogenisation by a central power. Switzerland, Belgium, Spain and Romania precisely do not have a unitary national culture at their disposal, and they thereby contradict the Romantic idea of a language-based community of people that organises itself into the form of a state. In Italy and Germany, a common national culture arose only after the unifications in the nineteenth century. In 1797, Schiller and Goethe had written in their collection of epigrams, *Xenien*: 'Germany? But where is that? I know not how to find the country; / Where the land of learning begins, the land of politics ends.'[2] The exclamation of a politician in the first session of the Italian parliament, in 1861, is also indicative: 'We have created Italy, now we must create Italians!'[3]

In order to substantiate the argument that Ukraine is split, reference is often made to the linguistic situation. But the Ukrainian and Russian languages are related; they both belong to the East Slavic branch of the Indo-Germanic family of languages. Ukrainian and Russian are linguistically about as far from one another as are Italian and Spanish. In Ukraine, both Ukrainian and Russian boast such a strong presence that most Ukrainians will understand each language without any problem. Both languages are used on television as well, and guests on talk shows often make use of whichever language is closer to them. A discussion can take place without further ado with Ukrainian responses to Russian questions, or the other way around; neither the participants in the discussion nor the members of the audience will perceive this situation of mixed languages as unnatural.

Bilingualism is found very widely, above all in the central regions of Ukraine. Speakers here casually switch from Ukrainian to Russian and back again, according to the given situation, and neither of the languages is discriminated against in daily usage.

A particular feature of Ukraine is a Ukrainian-Russian hybrid language called 'Surzhyk'. Originally *surzhyk* indicates a mixture of grains, made up of wheat and rye. There is no particular standard for this Surzhyk, so the proportion of Ukrainian and Russian elements may vary. Surzhyk can be a kind of Ukrainian that is stylised with reference to Russian, or a kind of Russian that is permeated with Ukrainian words. Among less well-educated speakers, indeed, it can happen that they cannot identify their own language correctly at all; sometimes speakers of Surzhyk are convinced that they are speaking Russian.

In Ukraine, the language question has always been a source of political strife. A law came into force on 28 October 1989 – thus prior to independence – that maintained its validity up until 2012. In the preamble, the official view is clearly formulated: 'The Ukrainian language is one of the important factors of the national authenticity of the Ukrainian people.' Furthermore, it is stated that Ukrainian should receive the status of official language, with the aim of 'supporting the comprehensive development of spiritual creative forces of the Ukrainian people and guaranteeing its sovereign national state future'.[4]

10 How many Ukraines are there?

With a Romantic view of things, national identity is here bound to the national language. Of course, the Ukrainian need to make anti-Russian distinctions plays a role too. Often the status of Ukrainian as unique official language is justified with the argument that Russian, historically dominant, would otherwise win the upper hand again. Moreover warnings are made that no Russian speaker would learn Ukrainian if it were not the unique official language of Ukraine.

The positive discrimination in favour of Ukrainian has in fact led to changes in the linguistic landscape. Ukrainian has gained prestige above all in the field of education and in public administration. This development is especially noticeable in the capital, Kyiv. In the 1990s, it was almost exclusively Russian that was spoken in Kyiv, whereas today Ukrainian clearly dominates, in writing as well as in spoken discourse.

In a survey carried out by the University of St Gallen in Spring 2013 a clear consensus could be seen in all regions that Ukrainian citizens should master Ukrainian (Figure 2.1).[5]

On the other hand, a clear gap emerged between East and West when it came to the question of whether Ukrainian citizens should master Russian (Figure 2.2).

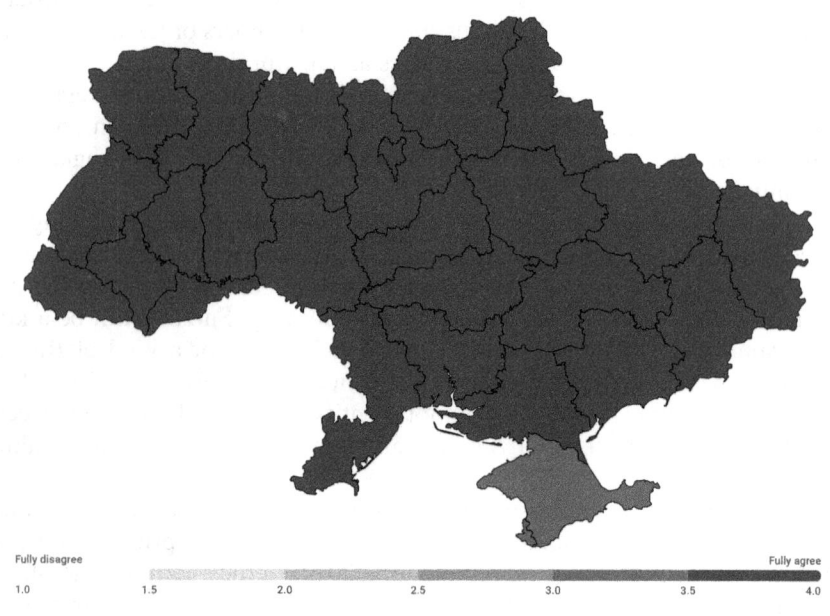

Figure 2.1 Do you agree that all inhabitants of Ukraine should master the Ukrainian language?
Note: mean value, 2013 survey.
Source: www.uaregio.org

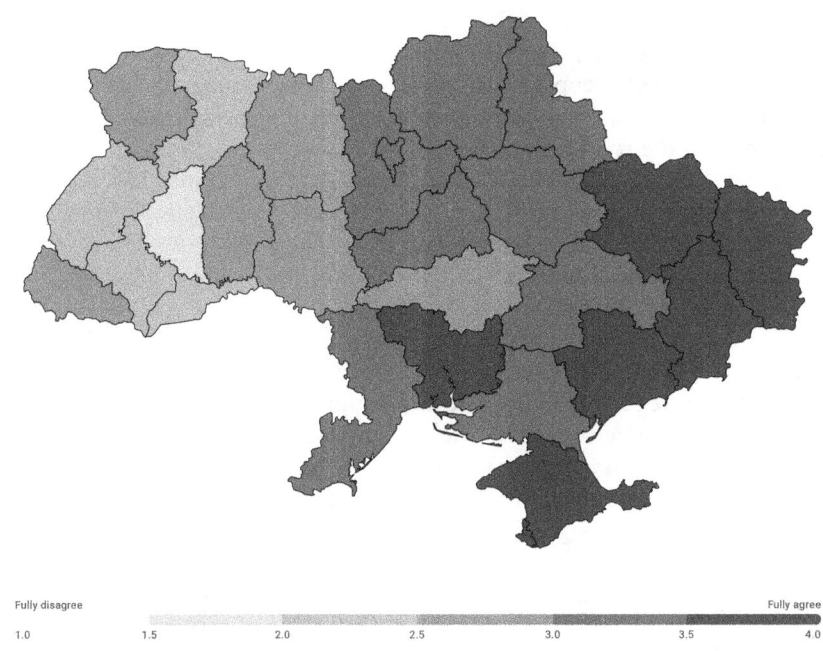

Figure 2.2 Do you agree that all inhabitants of Ukraine should master the Russian language?
Note: mean value, 2013 survey.
Source: www.uaregio.org

The individual presidents have pursued various goals – more or less Ukrainophile – in their language policies. At no point, though, did anyone question the status of Ukrainian as unique official language.

However, the law 'On the Foundations of Official Language Policies', signed by President Yanukovych in August 2012, represents a turning point. The provision of this law is that, in areas with a proportion of at least 10 per cent of speakers of a recognised minority language, an official regional language may then be introduced. As a result, Russian was elevated to the status of official regional language in 13 of the 27 regions of Ukraine. It is difficult to evaluate this law: on the one side, some account was taken of the linguistic reality in Ukraine, but, on the other side, with the introduction of Russian as the official regional language, there is a danger that the Ukrainian-speaking and Russian-speaking regions may drift further apart.

After President Yanukovych fled at the end of February 2014, one of the greatest mistakes of the Ukrainian rump parliament was to repeal this language law. There were protests as a result, above all in Eastern Ukraine; and the interim president, Oleksandr Turchynov, therefore suspended the decision that had been made by parliament.

Conversely, Russian was exploited by the separatists as an excellent way of marking political loyalty. At the climax of the drama in Sloviansk, in April 2014, the self-styled 'People's Mayor' Vyacheslav Ponomaryov called on the population to denounce suspicious traitors – and especially those speaking Ukrainian – to the rebel authorities.

In September 2017, a new bill on education was signed into law. According to the new regulation, Ukrainian will be the primary language of instruction at all school levels. Of course, the main goal of the new law is to promote a further cultural homogenisation of the young nation state. The official legitimation, however, drew on providing equal opportunities for all Ukrainian citizens, even for those with a different ethnic background. The Ministry of Education stated that the new law makes sure that people from all Ukrainian regions will have equal access to Ukrainian universities and will be eligible for public office or public service. Criticism has come mostly from neighbouring states, such as Hungary, Romania and Russia; the Council of Europe and the Venice Commission have also expressed concern about the possible negative consequences of a thorough Ukrainisation of the educational system. In 2018, the strict application of the law was somewhat softened. Private schools and public schools for national minorities will have some leeway to determine which subjects will be taught in the native language of the pupils.

In April 2019, the parliament passed a bill that affirms and promotes the official status of the state language even more. All Ukrainian citizens are now required to have a command of the Ukrainian language. All civil servants and state employees must use Ukrainian whenever they act in a professional capacity. Newspapers and magazines have to print at least 50 per cent of their content in Ukrainian. TV and radio stations need to broadcast 90 per cent of their shows in Ukrainian. The law even bans unconstitutional initiatives in favour of multilingualism as 'actions provoking division by language, ethnic conflict and hate'. The bill specifically aims to curb the use of Russian in Ukraine. In order not to jeopardise a future EU accession, Hungarian and Romanian are exempt from the new restrictions, and the Crimean Tatar language is awarded special status.

The question 'Ukrainian or Russian?' is hardly able to describe the complex reality of languages in Ukraine in an appropriate way. The last population census in Ukraine dates from 2001 (the next one was scheduled to take place in 2016 but was not carried out, due to the outbreak of war). In 2001, 67 per cent of citizens indicated that they spoke Ukrainian as their mother tongue, while barely 30 per cent spoke Russian as their mother tongue. The regional distribution of languages, though, was very varied. Ukrainian predominated in 22 of the 27 administrative districts – from 98 per cent in Ternopil, and 72 per cent in Kyiv, to 50 per cent in Zaporizhia. Conversely, the majority of the population in the regions of Luhansk, Donetsk and Crimea designated Russian as their mother tongue.

These data are problematic, though, since the concept of 'mother tongue' is not a good reflection of actual language use. The use of languages in the contexts of family and of work was collated in a survey from 2011. In the context of family, 47 per cent of those questioned gave Ukrainian as their preference, while 37 per cent gave Russian and 15 per cent gave both languages. Here too the regional differences were great. At work, of those questioned, 93 per cent used Ukrainian in the West as compared to 54 per cent in the Centre; while in the East and the South, Russian dominated at work with a score of 66 per cent. In the Centre of Ukraine, 6 per cent of those questioned switched from Ukrainian into Russian whenever they moved from a private context to a public context.[6]

One should therefore not assume that there are separated language areas in Ukraine, but rather that there is a linguistic continuum in which Ukrainian dominates in the West and Russian in the East. At the same time there will be family constellations or actual discursive situations in which both languages are employed next to one another in all regions of Ukraine. Those coloured maps of Ukraine in which language majorities are correlated with citizens' voting behaviour are especially liable to generate clichés. Western media often made use of such interpretative patterns for their explanations of Yanukovych's victory in the presidential elections of 2010: thus, the Ukrainian-speaking West had voted for Tymoshenko, while the Russian-speaking East had voted for Yanukovych. Such simplifications assume that there are clearly distinguishable cultural spaces in Ukraine with distinct political values. A consensus can be found in the whole of Ukraine, though, that human rights must be preserved and that omnipresent corruption must be fought.

After the Russian aggression in 2014, the situation changed again. Ukrainian nationals who predominantly speak Russian began to emphasise their 'Ukrainianness'. Their linguistic preference predicted their ethnic self-identification in a less distinct way. Support for and loyalty to the Ukrainian civic community increased.[7] It is clear that this process also changes the very category of 'Ukrainianness', which today is much broader than just an ethnolinguistic or national notion.[8]

The situation with regard to religious confessions turns out to be similarly complex. Whereas in Russia around 70 per cent of the population identify with Russian Orthodoxy, in Ukraine, there used to be three Orthodox Churches until 2019: (1) the Ukrainian Orthodox Church of the Moscow Patriarchate; (2) the Ukrainian Orthodox Church of the Kyiv Patriarchate; and (3) the Autocephalous Orthodox Church, which is closely associated with Constantinople. As well as the Orthodox Churches, there are also the Greek Catholic Church (rooted in Galicia above all), Roman Catholicism, and various forms of Protestantism, among which there are Baptists, Adventists, Lutherans, Mormons and Mennonites. These latter groups have adherents in the whole of Ukraine, with the exception of Galicia.

The most widespread is the Ukrainian Orthodox Church of the Moscow Patriarchate, with 37 per cent of all religious establishments, followed by various Protestant Churches, with 26 per cent, the Greek Catholic Church, with 14 per cent, the Orthodox Church of the Kyiv Patriarchate, with around 10 per cent, the Autocephalic Orthodox Church, with around 4 per cent, and finally the Roman Catholic Church, again with around 4 per cent.

The Ukrainian Orthodox Church of the Moscow Patriarchate was founded in 1990 as the legal successor to the Ukrainian Exarchate of the Russian Orthodox Church, and until recently it was the only canonical Church in Ukraine that was recognised by the Orthodox faith community. In 1992, a part of the clergy broke away and established the Ukrainian Orthodox Church of the Kyiv Patriarchate. The Autocephalous Ukrainian Orthodox Church, on the other hand, had already been established in 1921, when a separation of the Church from the Moscow Patriarchate was also on the agenda, carried along by Ukrainian demands for autonomy during the civil war. The Autocephalous Orthodox Church had adherents above all among Ukrainian emigrants, before they were officially recognised by the state in 1990.

For some time the Kyiv Patriarchate has been trying to position itself as the only true Orthodox Church in Ukraine. President Yushchenko had actively supported this plan, and indicated that the division of the Orthodox Church in Ukraine was a temporary matter. In fact, the three Orthodox Churches are often conceived by believers as a unity. The Church's allegiance to a Patriarchate does not in general disturb the religious practice of churchgoers. However, during and after the Euromaidan, attending services in a church that belongs to the Kyiv Patriarchate became a kind of political statement for Ukrainian patriots.

Tensions between the canonical Orthodox Church of the Moscow Patriarchate, on the one hand, and the two remaining orthodox churches, on the other, eventually increased. In October 2018, the Holy Synod in Constantinople declared that both the Ukrainian Orthodox Church of the Kyiv Patriarchate and the Autocephalous Orthodox Church are recognised in the orthodox community of the faithful. This decision triggered furious protests in Russia and enthusiastic applause in Ukraine. The Russian Duma condemned the Ukrainian 'schismatics', whereas President Poroshenko spoke about pushing the Ukrainian declaration of independence to the next stage. As an immediate reaction, the Russian Orthodox Church declared that it would not accept any decisions from Constantinople. The dispute over the canonical status of the Ukrainian Orthodox Church has far-reaching consequences. The Russian Orthodox Church is by far the most numerous among the 14 autocephalous orthodox churches that are recognised by the Holy Synod in Constantinople. In December 2018, a special council of 192 delegates (among them 64 bishops) met in St Sophia's Cathedral in Kyiv. They united the two orthodox branches that were critical of Moscow into one Orthodox Church of Ukraine, and 39-year-old Metropolitan Epifaniy was elected as head of the new church. Until then, Epifaniy (Serhii Dumenko) had been the right hand man of Patriarch Filaret of the Kyiv Patriarchate. On

Christmas Day, 6 January 2019, Epifaniy received the *tomos* (decree) granting independence to the newly established Orthodox Church in Ukraine from the hands of Ecumenical Patriarch Bartholomew of Constantinople. The political importance of this ceremony was highlighted by the presence of both President Poroshenko and former president Yushchenko.

Historically, the Orthodox Church has played a minor role in the formation of Ukrainian nationalism. Above all this has to do with the caesaropapism of Russian Orthodoxy, which recognised the hated Tsar as head of the Church. In Orthodoxy the principle of a *symphonia* ('accord') between secular and spiritual powers traditionally holds. Mykola Mikhnovsky (1873–1924) could thus write in his programmatic text *Independent Ukraine* (1900) that 'not only does a foreign Tsar rule over Ukraine, but God Himself has become a foreigner and knows no Ukrainian'.[9] Precisely because in the nineteenth century it was possible to conceive of Ukraine as merely a part of an overarching Russian nation, Orthodoxy was useless as far as modern efforts to achieve autonomy were concerned.

Circumstances looked quite different in the case of the Greek Catholic Church in Galicia, which, since the Church Union of Brest in 1596, has recognised the Roman Pope as head of the Church but which has kept the Orthodox rite. This confession, which spread mainly among the Ukrainians of Galicia (while the Poles naturally remained Roman Catholic), became an important component of a genuine Ukrainian identity. Furthermore, in the eighteenth and nineteenth centuries, the Greek Catholic religion protected many Ukrainians from Polonisation and Russification. During the Soviet period, the Greek Catholic Church was prohibited as an alleged breeding ground of Ukrainian nationalism. Both priests and believers were persecuted and sent to the Gulag. In this difficult time the Church may have shrunk in terms of its numbers, but it also consolidated itself spiritually. Today the remembrance of the martyrs from the time of Soviet dominance is kept alive in the Church. Although the Greek Catholic Church is only well established in the West and Centre of the country, it underlined its claim to have validity in the whole of Ukraine by relocating its episcopal see from Lviv to Kyiv in 2005.

In the process of forming a nation, though, the Greek Catholic religion collided with the Cossack myth, which honours the Ukrainian horsemen of the steppe as defenders of the Orthodox faith. The separatists in Donetsk, for instance, specifically invoke this Cossack tradition of Orthodoxy. In the preamble to the Constitution of the 'People's Republic of Donetsk' of 14 May 2014, they claim, grandiloquently, that they are 'part of the Russian world' and that they identify with the 'Orthodox belief (the Christian Orthodox belief of the Eastern confession) of the Russian Orthodox Church (of the Moscow Patriarchate), which represents the foundation of all foundations of the Russian world'.[10]

The opposition between the Greek Catholic Church and the Orthodox Church has concerned Ukrainians for a long time. The eminent historian,

Mykhailo Hrushevsky (1866–1934), who later became the first state president of the short-lived 'Ukrainian People's Republic', had already warned in 1906 about the fate of the Orthodox Serbs and the Catholic Croats, which in his view represented a frightening example of a people split along the lines of their religious confessions.

Both language and religion in Ukraine feature an opposition between West and East, but in neither case can a dividing line simply be drawn between two different cultures. The different linguistic, confessional and cultural traditions have not developed independently from each other but instead have often produced paradoxical contact phenomena. One example would be the enthusiasm for the Cossacks, for instance, which became widespread among the united Ukrainians in Austrian Galicia from the 1860s onwards.

Riabchuk's argument about the 'two Ukraines' thus falls short. The Lviv historian Yaroslav Hrytsak reacted to Riabchuk's conception with ironic derision; Hrytsak refers to the fundamental regional diversity of Ukraine and speaks provocatively of not just 'two' but rather of 'twenty-two Ukraines'.[11]

The results of more recent research have also shown that Ukraine cannot simply be subdivided into a pro-European West and a pro-Russian East. Although a Ukrainian national awareness is indeed sharply pronounced in the West, there is, however, no competing national identity facing it over in the East, but rather a value system that is still strongly rooted in Soviet traditions.

The image of a bisected Ukraine fails to take sufficient account of the complex, sometimes even contradictory realities at stake. In a survey in May 2013, the majority of the population in all regions thus believed in the necessity of building up good relations both with the EU and with Russia. Eastern and Western Ukraine were also in agreement in rejecting the corrupt presidency of Yanukovych. There was a consensus too with regard to maintaining the territorial unity of Ukraine. Even in Crimea, barely a year before its annexation, merely 23 per cent of those questioned expressed support for being incorporated into Russia, whereas 53 per cent advocated keeping the status quo (autonomy within Ukraine).[12]

Notes

1 Mykola Riabchuk, 'Two Ukraines Reconsidered: The End of Ukrainian Ambivalence?', *Studies in Ethnicity and Nationalism*, XV (2015), pp. 138–156.
2 Friedrich Schiller and Johann Wolfgang von Goethe, 'Das Deutsche Reich' (*Xenien*), in *Musenalmanach auf das Jahr 1797*, ed. Friedrich Schiller (Tübingen, 1797), p. 222. See Arndt Kremer, 'Transitions of a Myth? The Idea of a Language-Defined *Kulturnation* in Germany', *New German Review: A Journal of Germanic Studies*, XXVII/1 (2016), pp. 53–75.
3 See Stephanie Malia Hom, 'On the Origins of Making Italy: Massimo D'Azeglio and "Fatta l'Italia, bisogna fare gli Italiani"', *Italian Culture*, XXXI/1 (2013), pp. 1–16.
4 Bill Bowring, 'Law in a Linguistic Battlefield: The Language of the New State Versus the Language of the Oppressors in Ukraine?', *Language & Law*, I (2012), p. 5, available at: https://ssrn.com/abstract=2137831.

5 *Ukrainian Regionalism: A Research Platform*, available at: www.uaregio.org/en/surveys/methodology/.
6 Juliane Besters-Dilger, Kateryna Karunyk and Serhii Vakulenko, 'Language(s) in the Ukrainian Regions: Historical Roots and the Current Situation', in *Regionalism Without Regions: Reconceptualizing Ukraine's Heterogeneity*, ed. Ulrich Schmid and Oksana Myshlovska (Budapest, 2019), pp. 135–218.
7 Volodymyr Kulyk, 'Identity in Transformation: Russian-speakers in Post-Soviet Ukraine', *Europe-Asia Studies*, LXXI/1 (2019), pp. 156–178, doi:10.1080/09668136.2017.1379054.
8 Volodymyr Kulyk, 'Shedding Russianness, Recasting Ukrainianness: The Post-Euromaidan Dynamics of Ethnonational Identifications in Ukraine', *Post-Soviet Affairs*, XXXIV/2–3 (2018), pp. 119–138, doi:10.1080/1060586X.2018.1451232.
9 Catherine Wanner and Viktor Yelensky, 'Religion and the Cultural Geography of Ukraine', in *Regionalism Without Regions: Reconceptualizing Ukraine's Heterogeneity*, ed. Ulrich Schmid and Oksana Myshlovska (Budapest, 2019), pp. 247–296.
10 These elements were retroactively deleted on the official website of the 'People's Republic of Donetsk', available at: http://dnrsovet.su/zakonodatelnaya-deyatelnost/konstitutsiya. The original version is preserved at http://worldconstitutions.ru/?p=1094.
11 Yaroslav Hrytsak, 'Dvadtsiat dvi Ukrainy', in Yaroslav Hrytsak, *Strasti za natsionalizmom* (Kyiv, 2004), pp. 216–228; Yaroslav Hrytsak, 'On the Relevance and Irrelevance of Nationalism in Contemporary Ukraine', in *A Laboratory of Transnational History: Ukraine and Recent Ukrainian Historiography*, ed. Georgiy Kasianov and Philipp Ther (Budapest, 2009), pp. 225–248.
12 *Ukrainian Regionalism: A Research Platform*, available at: www.uaregio.org/en/surveys/data-visualisations/survey-infographics/.

3 The Russian perspective
'Little Russia' in the 'Russian World'

In a statement that created a sensation during the NATO summit in Bucharest in 2008, Putin described Ukraine as a 'very complicated state'.[1] On this occasion Putin reportedly even called Ukraine an 'artificial formation' and a 'mistake in history'.[2] Ukraine allegedly lacked a unified national consciousness, its territory had to a great extent been given to it by Russia, and moreover its state structures were in no way fully fledged. The Kremlin was here propagating an imperial vision whose origins lie in the nineteenth century. In Russian Romanticism, Ukraine was characterised as an Arcadia that to some extent lay just outside the Russian front door. Ukraine was thus considered not as an autonomous nation but rather as a 'Little Russia' that formed an indivisible whole together with 'Great Russia'.

Russia has always derived itself as a political entity from the first state, the so-called Kyivan Rus. This early medieval body politic experienced its high point in the tenth century; Kyiv became the most important centre of power in Eastern Europe. After its Christianisation in 988, Saint Sophia's Cathedral and the Monastery of the Caves were built there. The state was weakened in the middle of the twelfth century when the capital was transferred to Vladimir, the North Russian town, and ultimately it collapsed with the destruction of Kyiv in the Mongol invasion of 1240.

Not only Russian historiography but also Russian state symbolism today assume a tradition of dominance that leads from Kyivan Rus via the Grand Duchy of Moscow, the Tsarist Russia of the Romanovs and the Soviet empire directly to the Russian Federation. Ukrainian historians, meanwhile, interpret this process quite differently: for them, Kyivan Rus counts as the predecessor of the Ukrainian state. Between the twelfth and the twentieth centuries, Ukraine was then occupied by various other powers, and longest of all by Russia. With the independence of the Ukrainian state in 1991, in this view, the status quo ante was thus re-established.

The quarrel between these two factions is still not settled today. The virulence of these questions can be documented with reference to the erection of a new monument to Prince Vladimir in the city centre of Moscow on 4 November 2016. Prince Vladimir ruled over Kyivan Rus in the tenth century, and never visited Moscow – for the simple reason that Moscow did not exist at that time. The phantom pain of official Russia over the loss of Ukraine also has to be understood against this background. The break in the axis between Kyiv and Moscow in 1991 not only meant the secession of an important territory from Russia but also the loss of its entire early medieval national history. If Kyivan Rus drops out as a relevant chapter of historiography, then Russian history as such does not begin until the fourteenth century, with the victory of Grand Prince Dmitry Donskoy over the Mongols – which would mean a deep humiliation for the long tradition of a Russian statehood. Both in terms of political power and cultural bearing, the Kyivan Rus is much more important than the medieval principalities of Novgorod or Vladimir-Suzdal. With regard to its intensity, this debate over whether Kyivan Rus should belong to Russian or to Ukrainian history can only be compared to the so-called 'Viking dispute'; ever since the eighteenth century there has been a bitter argument in Russia over whether the 'Russians' descended from Scandinavian immigrants or whether they emerged from the autochthonous population.[3] The debate is still vibrant today. In 2016, a film with the programmatic title *Viking* was screened in Russian cinemas. The movie depicts the glorious battles of Prince Vladimir, who is assisted by Nordic mercenaries. Kyiv is shown as a gloomy, dark place that turns into a centre of civilisation only after the arrival of the Russian prince. The film was shot on locations in the newly annexed Crimea. The production and the content of the film form a unity that corroborates the alleged 1,000 years' history of Russian statehood.

It was only at the beginning of the nineteenth century that Ukraine entered Russian consciousness as a cultural space of its own. The beginning of modern Ukrainian literature is marked by a humorous text that transfers Virgil's *Aeneid* into the coarse language of the Ukrainian Cossack milieu; its author, Ivan Kotliarevsky (1769–1838), was a member of the landed gentry from Poltava, who as a theatre director in his hometown also wrote plays in Ukrainian. His *Eneyida*, which was published in 1798 in the capital, St Petersburg, together with explanatory vocabulary given in an appendix,[4] determined the way in which Ukrainian literature was received in Russia for the entire nineteenth century: everything that came from Ukraine was perceived as amusing and light-hearted entertainment, not making any deeper claims on the reader.[5]

Nikolai Gogol (1809–1852) also was able to exploit this horizon of expectation for the sake of his literary career. He had made his debut with the Romantic verse epic *Hans Küchelgarten* (1829), written in Russian,[6] but this had been a failure in critical terms. In the 1830s, he published two collections of short stories,[7] in which he not only took up Ukrainian themes but also adjusted his narrative style with reference to Ukrainian. Gogol still wrote these texts in Russian, but he distorted the syntax of the standard language and repeatedly interspersed his writing with Ukrainian terms – which, following Kotliarevsky's model, he explained to his 'Great Russian' readers in a glossary at the end of the volume. Moreover Gogol deployed just that sense of humour that his public expected in the context of Ukrainian local colour. The Russian national poet, Alexander Pushkin (1799–1837), in his review of

Gogol's Ukrainian stories, promptly made use of the cliché of a 'singing and dancing people' who can create folk art from the bounty of nature.[8] Apart from a brief note, Gogol himself wrote nothing in Ukrainian, and in 1844 he confessed in a famous passage in his letters: 'I myself do not know what kind of a soul I have – a Russian or a Ukrainian one.'[9]

While Gogol, as a Ukrainian writer, still moved entirely within the Russian horizon of expectation, around 1840, another author emerged who broke through this harmonious notion in a provocative way and consciously aspired to the position of a Ukrainian national poet. Taras Shevchenko was born as a serf in 1814. His lord of the manor, who may possibly have been his biological father, supported him and enabled him to study art in St Petersburg. His teacher, the painter Karl Bryullov (1799–1852), used the proceeds from one of his paintings to buy him his freedom. In 1846, in Kyiv, Shevchenko joined the Brotherhood of Saints Cyril and Methodius, together with Panteleimon Kulish (1819–1897) and Nikolay Kostomarov (1817–1885). During this period, Shevchenko wrote sharply satirical poems about Tsarist rule and lamented Ukraine's lack of freedom. Kostomarov composed a programmatic text for the Brotherhood of Saints Cyril and Methodius in which he sketched out – in both a Ukrainian and a Russian version – his audacious vision of a Pan-Slavic union under Ukrainian leadership:

> For the voice of Ukraine has not fallen silent. And Ukraine will be resurrected from her grave and will address her Slavic brothers, and her call will be heard, and the Slavic culture will be resurrected, and there will be no Tsar, no Tsarevich, no Prince, no Count and no Duke any more, and there will be no more Excellencies, no more Lords, no more Boyars, no more peasants and no more serfs – neither in Muscovy nor in Poland nor in Ukraine nor in Czechia nor in Slovenia, nor among the Serbs or among the Bulgars. Ukraine will be an independent republic in a Slavic federation. Then all the peoples of the earth will be able to point to that place on the map where Ukraine is marked: for behold, the stone here that the builders rejected has now become the cornerstone.[10]

The Biblical style here and the allusion to the Gospel of Matthew (21:42) are of course intentional, and they underline the claim to truth of this conception – in which socialist undertones also resonate.

The Brotherhood, whose alignment was more Romantic than revolutionary, was broken up in 1847, following a denunciation. Kostomarov and Kulish escaped comparatively unscathed, but Shevchenko, on the other hand, was sent into exile in Kazakhstan to do military service for ten years, deprived of the right to exercise his art. How little sympathy his fate elicited even among progressive-thinking Russian intellectuals can be seen in an exemplary way in the reaction of the influential literary critic Vissarion Belinsky (1811–1848). In a letter, Belinsky commented on the imprisonment of the Ukrainian poet with quite explicit gloating:

Sound common sense has to see in Shevchenko a donkey, an idiot and a villain – and furthermore a drunkard, a vodka-lover with a patriotic Ukrainian vein ... Shevchenko has been banished to the Caucasus, as a soldier. I do not feel sorry for him; and if I had been his judge, I would have sentenced him to no less than this. I harbour a personal enmity towards his sort of liberals ... With their brazen stupidities these people provoke the Government, arouse their mistrust and lead them to see a revolt where there is nothing at all.[11]

When Shevchenko was finally released, in 1857, he returned to St Petersburg. His health had been ruined, though, and in 1861 he died in the Russian capital. Subsequently, Kostomarov and Kulish pursued the canonisation of the poet with diligence, Shevchenko being seen as the incarnation of Ukrainian national consciousness. The most important medium for this project was the short-lived journal *Osnova*, which came out in St Petersburg between 1861 and 1862, and was devoted to Ukrainian culture in an encyclopaedic manner. Together with contributions on Ukrainian history and folklore, pieces of agronomic or legal advice could also be found here, intended for lords of the manor in the province. The biography and the œuvre of Shevchenko occupied prominent positions in the journal. *Osnova* published Shevchenko's diary, which he had written in Russian, as well as numerous poems and works in Ukrainian; literary reminiscences of the national poet were also printed here. In the individual numbers of the journal, Kulish published a *Survey of Ukrainian Literature*, written in Russian, and thereby sought to reinforce the claim of Ukraine to cultural autonomy.

For the assertion of a Ukrainian nation, first and foremost, a Ukrainian language and a Ukrainian literature were called for. In making this assumption, Ukrainian intellectuals could invoke the famous chapter about the Slavs in *Outlines of a Philosophy of the History of Man* (1791) by Johann Gottfried Herder (1744–1803). Herder declared that language was the most important foundation of the national character of a people, and he promised the Slavic peoples that one day they 'will at length awake from their long and heavy slumber, shake off the chains of slavery, [and] enjoy the possession of their delightful lands'.[12]

In *Osnova*, Nikolay Kostomarov also published his important essay 'Two Russian Nationalities'.[13] Kostomarov proposed an interpretation with a harmonising effect: Russian-ness thus appeared in both 'Great Russian' and 'Little Russian' variants. The former was responsible for the formation of a state, whereas the latter had to provide the basis of culture, and therefore both peoples depended on one another and supplemented one another in an ideal way.

Kulish defended an approach that was similar to that of Kostomarov. He had already referred to the fact that the Ukrainian and the Russian languages have a common foundation at their disposal in the Russian-language afterword to his novel *The Black Council* (1857).[14] Kulish was thereby trying to deflect suspicion about Ukrainian separatism away from his project, but at the same time to provide justification for the existence of a Ukrainian literature in the Tsarist Empire, given the dominant Russian culture of the latter. Even with this limited conception, however, Kulish found himself on a collision course with the Tsarist authorities. Until around 1840, a political dimension had not been ascribed to Ukrainian culture either in Russia or in Ukraine itself. In the nineteenth century, the loose cannons in Russia were, above all, the Poles. A revolt had already erupted in the Russian Partition of Poland in 1830, a revolt that was bloodily suppressed. After this experience, the Russian central powers tried to draw the Ukrainians to their side: in 1834, the Kyiv Imperial University of Saint Vladimir was founded, the naming of which already referred back to the famous Prince of Kyivan Rus and thus underlined the unity of Ukraine and Russia.

It was not until the Shevchenko affair that a political 'Ukraine question' emerged from 'Little Russian' culture; and at first, attempts were made to get rid of this problem by evoking the common ethnic identity of Russians and Ukrainians.

Meanwhile, though, the Poles represented a continuous source of unrest. When the Polish January Uprising erupted in 1863, the Russian authorities reacted with harsh repression. The leaders of the uprising were executed, many Polish noblemen were despatched to Siberia, the name of Poland itself was outlawed and replaced by the label 'Vistula Land', and henceforth school teaching took place in Russian only. The Russian Government now did everything in its power to ensure that Ukrainian patriots would not end up in the separatist channel that the Poles had taken; so in Ukraine too, after the carrot, it was now decided to use the stick. In 1863, the conservative Russian Minister of the Interior, Pyotr Valuyev sent out a circular which limited the printing of Ukrainian books to works of fiction. In this decree the famous statement can be found claiming that 'the majority of Little Russians themselves' believe, with good reason, that 'a Little Russian language has not [existed], does not, and cannot exist, and that its dialects as spoken by the masses are the same as the Russian language, with the exception of some corruptions from Poland'.[15] In 1876, the so-called Ems Decree (*Ukaz*) of Tsar Alexander II sharpened the criteria for the publication of Ukrainian works even further. It was not until 1905 that the Russian Academy of Sciences recognised Ukrainian as a separate language.

It is indicative that Valuyev carefully avoided the very concept of 'Ukrainian'. In the nineteenth century, the Tsarist authorities attempted to define Ukraine either as 'Little Russia' or, even better, simply as 'South Russia'. In the largely Tsarist *Brockhaus and Efron Encyclopedic Dictionary* that appeared between 1890 and 1907, the substantive entry on Ukrainian literature was to be found under the heading 'South Russian Literature'. Under the heading 'Ukraine', this reference work cautiously advanced the following: 'The South-Eastern Russian territories of the *Rzeczpospolita* [Commonwealth] called themselves this; but the name was never official and was used only in private social interactions, finding its way into folk poetry.'[16]

'Little Russia' originally indicated the Cossack Hetmanate east of the Dnieper river. After the Polish partitions, the name was also extended to cover the right-bank (western) areas. The concept 'Little Russia' was used to emphasise that Ukraine together with White Russia (Belarus) and Great Russia formed an indivisible Russian empire. In this context, though, the way in which the Hetmanate was integrated into the Russian empire has remained controversial ever since. In 1654, the Cossack leader (*Hetman*) Bohdan Khmelnytsky had entered into an agreement with the Russian Tsar, in Pereyaslav, that assured him of assistance against the hostile Poles. Even today, in modern historical works, this agreement is interpreted in different ways by Russians and by Ukrainians. Russian interpretations thus point to the belief that the Pereyaslav agreement founded a real – or at least a personal – union between Russia and Ukraine. This point of view reached its culmination in the Soviet version of events. In 1954, the 300th anniversary of the 'reunification' of Russia and Ukraine was celebrated; in this context, the Pereyaslav agreement appeared as the recovery of a previous unity that had been interrupted by the foreign rule of the Poles. By way of contrast, Ukrainian historians tend to believe that the Pereyaslav agreement was originally just a pact concerning military assistance which was later misused by the Tsars in order to legitimize the extension of their power over Ukraine. Catherine the Great (1729–1796) certainly has the worst image of all Russian rulers, from the Ukrainian perspective; in 1775, she abolished the prerogatives of the Cossacks and implemented a standardised bureaucratic organisation of the Empire.

The Ukrainian Cossack myth is derived from this conflict – a myth that is still alive today. According to this myth, the Russians are seen as representatives of an autocratic system, whereas the old Cossack order is glorified as being liberal and democratic. The Tsarist order refused for a long time to see an independent national culture in Ukraine; meanwhile, conversely, Ukrainian intellectuals articulated their positions more and more clearly. An important voice belonged to Mykhailo Drahomanov (1841–1895), who took it upon himself to be 'a European liberal and a socialist with a Ukrainian basis'.[17] Drahomanov turned against the narrow-mindedness of Ukrainian nationalists who may have rejected Russian literature merely because it was written in Russian. In contrast to such nationalists, he maintained that Russian literature was in fact much more European and politically more progressive than Ukrainian literature. In his texts, Drahomanov formulated the vision of a democratic Ukraine in a liberal Europe; and here he was not on a collision course with Russia but wanted rather to embed Ukraine in a 'free federation' with its great neighbour. The Russian authorities themselves wanted nothing to do with such moderate views, and in 1875 they forced Drahomanov to resign from his Chair at the Kyiv Imperial University. From 1876 to 1889, he lived in Geneva, where he ran an *Imprimerie ukrainienne* and published his journal *Hromada*. In 1889, Drahomanov relocated to Sofia, where he remained active as Professor of History until his death.

Mykola Mikhnovsky (1873–1924) took up a position much more radical than that of Drahomanov. In his manifesto, *Independent Ukraine* (1900), Mikhnovsky demanded a sovereign Ukrainian state 'from the Carpathians to the Caucasus' with Ukrainian as its state language.[18] He adopted a radical anti-Russian position and, in 1904, even attempted to blow up a statue of Pushkin in Kharkiv. This attack on a monument to the Russian national poet was supposed to make clear that Russian culture had no place in Ukraine and should indeed be destroyed.

Mikhnovsky's action, though, was not well received by the local population. In Tsarist Ukraine, a pro-Russian attitude predominated. The Government in St Petersburg nonetheless overestimated Ukrainians' loyalty – above all, in non-Russian areas. At the beginning of the First World War, Russian troops occupied Austrian East Galicia and promptly began a process of Russification there. However, they were soon met by bitter resistance, and the Russians were certainly not received with open arms. Ukrainian national consciousness had been able to develop much further under the comparatively liberal conditions of the Habsburg Empire than in the Ukraine that was under Russian rule.

The collapse of the Tsarist Empire brought a brief period of sovereign statehood for Ukraine. However, no government was able to sustain itself for long. The project of a sovereign Ukrainian state failed, because too many protagonists with different agendas clashed with each other and because too many covetous foreign eyes were directed towards Ukraine. After the abdication of the Tsar in February 1917, a central council in Kyiv had attempted to establish a 'Ukrainian People's Republic' (UNR). The respected historian Mykhailo Hrushevsky (1866–1934) was elected as President. Hrushevsky tried straight away to take account of the regional diversity of Ukraine, and proposed that the country be divided into thirty districts and that three cities (Kyiv, Kharkiv and Odessa) be given special status.

As a result of the October Revolution, in 1917, the Bolsheviks took power in Russia. After strenuous efforts, Lenin managed to convince his comrades of the absolute necessity of making peace with Germany. The price for this, as brokered in the peace negotiations with Germany in Brest-Litovsk on 3 March 1918, consisted in the surrender of enormous territories in the West of Russia – among them, Ukraine. The Germans then installed a puppet regime in Kyiv under Hetman Pavlo Skoropadskyi (1873–1945). With his conservative social policies and his closeness to the German Empire, however, he enjoyed little support among the population. Skoropadskyi was overthrown as early as November 1918 by a directorate under the leadership of the poet Volodymyr Vynnychenko (1880–1951), who had a social-revolutionary outlook, and Symon Petliura (1879–1926), who had a nationalistic disposition. For a short time the directorate again restored the Ukrainian People's Republic (UNR). The greatest success of the directorate consisted in uniting with the 'West Ukrainian People's Republic' (ZUNR), which had arisen on the basis of the former Austrian territories of Ukraine. The date, 22 January

1919, is counted as the foundation day of the so-called *sobornist*, the unity of Western and Eastern Ukraine. *Sobornist* is a concept that originally derives from Orthodox theology and that signifies the claim to unification of the Church. In this context, *sobornist* refers precisely not to the unity guaranteed by state rule and bureaucracy, but rather to a voluntary community achieved by means of spiritual affinities. There was also a commemoration of this intra-Ukrainian unification in 1990 when, before the anniversary of the *sobornist*, a human chain was formed connecting Lviv with Kyiv. Since 1999, in fact, 22 January has been a public holiday in the state of Ukraine. The principle of *sobornist* is also laid down in the current Constitution of 1996: Article 2 determines that Ukraine is a unitary state.

In 1919, though, the unity of Western and Eastern Ukraine could not be maintained for long in the face of military reality. Symon Petliura formed an alliance with the new Polish head of state, Józef Piłsudski (1867–1935), in which he secured Polish military support against the Red Army; in return, Petliura recognised Polish territorial claims to the former Austrian West Ukraine (Galicia and Volhynia). The leaders of the ZUNR were naturally appalled by this plan and felt that Petliura had betrayed them, so they withdrew from the joint state-building project. In the end, Petliura's gambit helped neither of the two Ukrainian state entities. The Bolsheviks, meanwhile, were slowly but surely winning the upper hand. After the victory of the Red Army, the Ukrainian Soviet Socialist Republic was founded towards the end of 1919; until 1934 its capital was Kharkiv, and thereafter Kyiv.

During the Soviet period, the Communist Party did everything it could to discredit the brief intermezzo of Ukrainian statehood after the First World War as a German conspiracy against Russia and as a proto-fascist undertaking. In *Shchors* (1939), for instance, the historicising propaganda film by Alexander Dovzhenko, the border signs of the UNR are thus written in German, and Petliura here resembles Adolf Hitler in his physiognomy and rhetoric to an almost obtrusive extent.

After the civil war the Soviet Government wanted to portray itself as the opposite of the Tsarist Empire in all areas of political life. The Bolsheviks claimed that they had put an end to the Tsarist prison house of peoples. Lenin himself defended the national pride of the Great Russians, but wanted to purify this pride and prevent it from being associated with the imperialist suppression of smaller peoples – and here he also explicitly named the Ukrainians. Russian national pride had to be focused on the socialist achievements of one's own people. In the first government of the Bolsheviks, Stalin was responsible for such questions as the People's Commissar for Nationalities. In 1925, he issued the following slogan: Soviet culture must be 'nationalist in form and socialist in content'.[19]

At first, it seemed as if Ukraine could profit from this progressive political approach to nationalities. In the 1920s, the government in the Kremlin attempted to encourage acceptance of the Communist system by means of installing local cadres in offices of state. This policy of *korenizatsiya* (literally, 'putting down roots') led to a massive rise in the number of Ukrainian members in the Ukrainian party leadership. The noble promises, though, were soon overtaken by the savage reality. The two party politicians Alexander Shumsky (1890–1946) and Mykola Skrypnyk (1872–1933) had advocated a Bolshevism with Ukrainian characteristics. Both of them were removed from their posts by Stalin because of their tendency towards a nationalist communism; Shumsky was arrested in 1933 and condemned to ten years in a prison camp, while Skrypnyk was driven to commit suicide.[20]

A great many Ukrainian writers and artists who had contributed to the so-called 'Ukrainian renaissance' in the 1920s were also politically repressed. Mykola Khvylovy (1893–1933) was a staunch communist who participated in the violent revolutionary events of the civil war. His impressive literary works were also a kind of self-therapy for his traumatised ego. In the story *Me (Romance)* of 1924, for example, a Cheka officer sentences his own mother to death for the sake of communist ideals. In 1933, Khvylovy committed suicide after a close friend, the Futurist poet Mykhailo Yalovy (1895–1937), had been arrested. Many outstanding Ukrainian intellectuals perished in 1937 in Sandarmokh, a forest in Karelia. The avant-garde writers Mykola Kulish (1892–1937) and Maik Yohansen (1895–1937), the novelist Valerian Pidmohylny (1901–1937), and the theatre director Les Kurbas (1887–1937) all faced Stalin's execution squads.

Astonishingly, after this brutal disciplining, Ukraine did not develop into a source of smouldering unrest, but rather into an important stage in several successful Communist biographies. Nikita Khrushchev (1894–1971), Nikolai Podgorny (1903–1983) and Leonid Brezhnev (1906–1982) completed significant stages of their careers in Ukraine, which in the unofficial hierarchy of Soviet republics was always counted as *secunda inter pares* after Russia. Conditions in Ukraine were stable, thus supporting the political stagnation of the Brezhnev period. This could be seen not least in the long periods of office of the Soviet functionaries Petro Shelest (1908–1996) and Volodymyr Shcherbytsky (1918–1990), who led the Ukrainian party organisation from 1963–1972 and 1972–1989 respectively.

The promotion of Ukrainian culture was also tolerated by the Soviet Union as long as Kyiv kept to the prescriptions of Moscow – and the loyalty of Ukraine to the Communist project could hardly be doubted. In 1968, Shelest was one of the most vehement advocates of a military intervention in the Prague Spring. Shelest himself demonstrated what a Soviet-compatible Ukrainian nationalism might look like in his effusively written book with the pathos-laden title *O Ukraine, Our Soviet Land* (1970).[21] However, the Ukrainophile Shelest was replaced in 1972 by the apparatchik Shcherbytsky, who even during the period of *perestroika* still stubbornly clung to the principles of the administrative command economy. Shcherbytsky, who himself strictly spoke only Russian, followed a neo-Stalinist cultural policy. In 1978, the Ukrainian Ministry of Education issued an instruction that Russian must strictly be enforced as the language of teaching in schools. Towards the end of the Stalin era, as many as 81 per cent of pupils had been going to Ukrainian-speaking schools, but by the end of the 1980s, this proportion had shrunk to 47.5 per cent.[22]

When in 1990 it became ever clearer that it would be impossible to maintain the Soviet Union as such, the project of a federation of the individual Soviet republics was initially up for discussion. In this question it was decisive how Ukraine would vote; and the vote soon turned out, with complete clarity, to be negative and in favour of an independent state instead. The relation to Russia was tense from the very beginning, since Moscow was laying claim to a leadership role and threatening to adjust the relevant boundaries as well. This concerned Crimea and Sevastopol above all, where the Russian Black Sea Fleet was stationed.

Quite apart from these strategic disputes, the Ukrainian claims to autonomy caught both the general Russian population and numerous intellectuals completely unawares. Many Russians still believed in the Soviet illusion of a friendship between peoples in general and in a Ukrainian-Russian brotherhood in particular; even in their wildest dreams they could not have imagined that Kyiv would turn its back on Moscow. The harshest statements in this situation did not come from notorious Russian nationalists but rather from former dissidents, such as Aleksandr Solzhenitsyn (1918–2008) and Joseph Brodsky (1940–1996).

In 1991, Brodsky wrote a sarcastic poem with the title 'On Ukrainian Independence'.[23] In this poem he disparagingly and scornfully discusses Ukraine's aspirations to cultural autonomy, and holds the view that Ukraine quite categorically belongs to the Great Russian cultural space. This position finds its most lucid and emphatic expression in the gloating final lines of the poem:

> But mark: when it's your turn to be dragged to graveyards,
> You'll whisper and wheeze, your deathbed mattress a-pushing,
> Not Taras' bullshit but poetry lines from Alexander.

The reference here is of course to the Russian national poet Alexander Pushkin, who for Russians counts as 'our everything', and, on the other hand, to his counterpart Taras Shevchenko, who stands at the centre of Ukrainian national culture.

In 1994, Solzhenitsyn gave an interview to *Forbes* magazine in which he stated that Ukraine in her present borders possesses territories that historically belonged to Russia:

> In 1919, when he imposed his regime on Ukraine, Lenin gave her several Russian provinces to assuage her feelings. These provinces have never historically belonged to Ukraine. I am talking about the eastern and southern territories of today's Ukraine. Then, in 1954, Khrushchev, with the arbitrary capriciousness of a satrap, made a 'gift' of the Crimea to Ukraine.[24]

In Ukraine, such comments naturally confirmed all the prejudices about Great Russian cultural imperialism, against which one should stand with the utmost force. In the 1990s, the need for Russia to be kept at a distance could be seen above all in the debates about the Ukrainian constitution which finally came into force in 1996. In its preamble, the traditional subject of enunciation in a constitution, namely, 'We the people', announced itself in a double sense: as 'the Ukrainian people' and also as 'citizens of Ukraine of all nationalities'. Article 10 elevated Ukrainian to become the official language. At the same time, though, 'the free development, the use and the protection of the Russian language and of other languages of the national minorities of Ukraine' was guaranteed.

Leonid Kuchma was the President of Ukraine from 1994 to 2004. In 2003, he published a book with the programmatic title *Ukraine Is Not Russia*.[25] Kuchma here criticised the hegemony of Russia in the Soviet Union: the Russians had thus taken too little notice of the other nationalities, which in the end had led to the collapse of the multi-ethnic Soviet state. He also held the position that it was too soon to introduce Russian as a second official language in Ukraine. Similarly, Mykola Riabchuk has likened the relationship between Ukraine and Russia to Canada's neighbourly relations with the USA. He quotes Premier Pierre Trudeau who, in 1969, compared his country's situation to sleeping in a bed together with an elephant: thus, even if your bedfellow is peaceful, you will sense every movement.[26]

The so-called Orange Revolution of 2004 then marked a sharp incision in relations between Russia and Ukraine. The street protests against the fraudulent election of Viktor Yanukovych were understood by the Russian Government as a direct threat to its own internal political stability. The Kremlin reacted to the demonstrations in Kyiv with an intensification of its propaganda, which was expressed most clearly in the foundation of the patriotic youth movement 'Our People'. This organisation was formally launched in 2005, and its first public appearance was on a symbolic date, namely, the sixtieth anniversary of the victory over Hitler's Germany. Over 60,000 young people submerged the streets of Moscow under a sea of banners. With this staged demonstration the idea was to make sure that the young generation in Russia would not develop into a critical force in public life, but would rather remain bound to the centrally managed nationalistic project of the Kremlin.[27] However, the outreach to the Russian youth did not prove to be sustainable, as the massive student protests in Moscow in March 2017 showed.

In 2007, Putin started a charm offensive and offered the government in Kyiv the opportunity to celebrate the 300th anniversary of the Battle of Poltava (1709) together. The offer was a devious one: for the Russians, the victory over the enemy Swedes at Poltava signifies the beginning of the imperial era, whereas the Ukrainians see in this battle an attempt to secure their independence from Russia with Swedish assistance. Judgements of Hetman Ivan Mazepa (1639–1709) also differ massively in this context. As a literary figure, Mazepa haunts the work of Alexander Pushkin, Lord Byron, Gottfried Keller and Bertolt Brecht. From a Russian point of view, Mazepa is a traitor who defected to the Swedes, whereas, from a Ukrainian point of view, he is a hero who put his life at stake for the national cause. In any case, Viktor Yushchenko, the President of Ukraine at the time, did not accept Putin's offer and instead signed a decree with the baroque title 'On the Commemoration of the 300th Anniversary of the Events Concerning the Ukrainian Hetman Mazepa and the Alliance that was Concluded Between Ukraine and Sweden During the Great Northern War'. Yushchenko ordered that streets be renamed and that monuments be set up for Mazepa and for the Swedish King Charles XII. He even considered establishing a Swedish-Ukrainian historical commission. Viktor Chernomyrdin (1938–2010), the Russian Ambassador to Kyiv at the time, protested vigorously and compared the plan for a monument to Charles XII in Poltava to the absurdity of setting up a monument to Hitler in Stalingrad.

From Putin's viewpoint, Ukraine is important in many different ways. First of all, the Kremlin is reliant on a loyal Ukraine for its delivery of energy supplies to Western Europe. Debates over Russian gas prices in Ukraine end, with a fine regularity, with the threat that Moscow might turn off the tap or that Kyiv in return might help itself to gas supplies intended for Western Europe. Such skirmishes damage Russia's reputation as a reliable energy supplier and will lead the West further to diversify its energy mix. The Kremlin is also looking for new customers, and is constructing the pipeline 'Power of Siberia' which is supposed to supply China with Russian gas. Moreover, Gazprom is putting considerable effort into the construction of alternative gas routes to Europe, bypassing Ukraine, such as Nord Stream and TurkStream. Since 2016, Ukraine has not been buying the gas needed for its own consumption directly from Russia but partially in reverse flow from EU member states.

Ukraine has also been courted geopolitically by Moscow in what by now has become a very one-sided kind of love. Ever since the demise of the Soviet Union, the Kremlin has considered the 'near abroad' as its own sphere of influence.[28] Putin would like to bring a 'Eurasian Union' into being that could then operate in both political and commercial terms on an equal footing with the EU, the USA, China and Japan. By means of such a Eurasian Union, an important step would be completed in the direction of that multipolar world order that the Kremlin envisions as the ideal organisational form of the international community of states.

It was precisely the cultural proximity of Ukraine – according to Russian propaganda – that induced the Russian Government to forego open aggression (as in the *Blitzkrieg* that was unleashed against Georgia in August 2008). The Kremlin decided to stage a 'hybrid war' instead; so the territory to be captured was not officially occupied but rather infiltrated by soldiers operating without insignia, while at the same time an army stood ready for action at the border and thus served as a background threat. The US historian Timothy Snyder has characterised the Russian aggression in Ukraine as 'reverse asymmetrical warfare',[29] meaning that it simulates a traditional asymmetrical war in which a militarily weaker combatant attacks a superior opponent using guerrilla tactics. While it is obvious that Russia is militarily stronger than Ukraine, Russia thus nonetheless simulates an asymmetrical war whereby it is the Ukrainian army that, at least at first sight, is made to appear the stronger power. The Russian Government does not want to admit that it is itself a combatant, preferring instead to define the conflict as a Ukrainian civil war. So the separatists are defending themselves against the Ukrainian army – except that, behind the separatists, there stands a massive Russian commitment in terms of soldiers, weapons and supplies.

Given the annexation of Crimea and the simulated civil war in Eastern Ukraine, political relations between Russia and Ukraine have relapsed in a very short time by more than a hundred years. From a Ukrainian point of view, Russia appears once again a dangerous imperialistic power against which one must defend oneself with all the means at one's disposal. After the events of Spring 2014, there was thus a majority in Ukraine in favour of joining NATO. In 2008, by comparison, when the government led by Yushchenko had been making the case that Ukraine should become a member of the Western military alliance, there had been no broad support for such a project among the population.

Admittedly, the official rhetoric of the Kremlin still talks about the 'brother peoples' of Russia and Ukraine. Such clichés, though, sound merely hollow to the ears of most Ukrainians. Indeed, the Kremlin policy of not even preserving an appearance of plausibility in its lies about the war has driven many Ukrainian citizens who had previously defined themselves as ethnic Russians into the arms of Kyiv. Moscow's aggressive Ukraine policies have ultimately achieved just the opposite of their original aim, and the double assault on Crimea and in Donbas has strengthened Ukrainian statehood instead of breaking it up. In the course of 2014, a surge of national consensus took hold not only of Western Ukraine but also of those regions that traditionally were not markedly inclined to patriotism.

Notes

1 Text of Putin's speech at NATO Summit, Bucharest, 2 April 2008, available at: www.unian.info/world/111033-text-of-putins-speech-at-nato-summit-bucharest-april-2-2008.html.
2 'At 2008 NATO-Russia Council, Putin Called Ukraine "Artificial Formation" and "Mistake in History" – Linkevicius', *UNIAN*, 7 December 2018, available at: www.unian.info/politics/10368393-at-2008-nato-russia-council-putin-called-ukraine-artificial-formation-and-mistake-in-history-linkevicius.html.
3 Knud Rahbek Schmidt, 'The Varangian Problem: A Brief History of the Controversy', in *Varangian Problems*, ed. Knud Hannestad (Copenhagen, 1970), pp. 7–20.
4 Ivan Kotliarevsky, *Eneïda* (Kharkiv, 2011); see Kotliarevsky, *Aeneid*, trans. Bohdan Melnyk (Toronto, 2004).
5 George Grabowicz, 'Subversion and Self-Assertion: The Role of *Kotliarevshchyna* in Russian-Ukrainian Literary Relations', in *History of the Literary Cultures of East-Central Europe: Junctures and Disjunctures in the 19th and 20th Centuries*, ed. Marcel Cornis-Pope and John Neubauer (Amsterdam, 2004), vol. I, pp. 401–408.
6 See Nikolai Gogol, *Hanz Kuechelgarten*, in Gogol, *Hanz Kuechelgarten, Leaving the Theater and Other Works*, trans. Ronald Meyer (Ann Arbor, MI, 1990).

7 See Nikolai Gogol, *Village Evenings Near Dikanka and Mirgorod*, trans. Christopher English (Oxford, 1994).
8 See Roman Koropeckyj and Robert Romanchuk, 'Ukraine in Blackface: Performance and Representation in Gogol's *Dikan⊠ka Tales*, Book 1', *Slavic Review*, LXII/3 (2003), pp. 525–547.
9 George S. N. Luckyj, *Between Gogol and Shevchenko* (Munich, 1971), p. 123.
10 Thomas Michael Prymak, *Mykola Kostomarov: A Biography* (Toronto, 1996), p. 49.
11 Victor Swoboda, 'Shevchenko and Belinsky', in *Shevchenko and the Critics*, ed. George S. N. Luckyj (Toronto, 1980), pp. 303–323.
12 Johann Gottfried von Herder, *Outlines of a Philosophy of the History of Man*, trans. T. Churchill (New York, 1966), pp. 483–484.
13 *Fashioning Modern Ukraine: Selected Writings of Mykola Kostomarov, Volodymyr Antonovych and Mykhailo Drahomanov*, ed. Serhiy Bilenky (Toronto, 2013), pp. 131–174.
14 Panteleimon Kulish, *The Black Council*, trans. George S. N. and Moira Luckyj (Littleton, CO, 1973).
15 'The Valuyev Decree', in Paul Robert Magocsi, *A History of Ukraine: The Land and Its Peoples*, 2nd edn (Toronto, 2010), pp. 393–394.
16 'Ukraina', in *Entsiklopedicheskii slovar' Brokgauza i Efrona* (St Petersburg, 1902), vol. XXXIV, pp. 633–635.
17 Ivan L. Rudnytsky, *Essays in Modern Ukrainian History*, ed. Peter L. Rudnytsky (Edmonton, 1987), pp. 203–254.
18 Mykola Mikhnovsky, *Independent Ukraine: Programme of the Ukrainian Revolutionary Party from 1900* (London, 1967).
19 See Yuri Slezkine, 'The USSR as a Communal Apartment, or How a Socialist State Promoted Ethnic Particularism', *Slavic Review*, LIII/2 (1994), pp. 414–452.
20 George O. Liber, *Total Wars and the Making of Modern Ukraine, 1914–1954* (Toronto, 2016), pp. 169–200.
21 See Lowell Tillett, 'Ukrainian Nationalism and the Fall of Shelest', *Slavic Review*, XXXIV/4 (1975), pp. 752–768.
22 Taras Kuzio, *Ukraine: Democratization, Corruption, and the New Russian Imperialism* (Santa Barbara, CA, 2015), pp. 25f.
23 Joseph Brodsky, 'On Ukrainian Independence', trans. Artem Serebrennikov, in Sergey Armeyskov, *Russian Universe: Understanding Russia with a Russian*, available at: https://russianuniverse.org/2017/02/27/joseph-brodsky-on-ukrainian-independence (accessed 27 February 2017).
24 'Alexander Solzhenitsyn on the New Russia', *Forbes*, 5 August 2008, available at: www.forbes.com/2008/08/05/solzhenitsyn-forbes-interview-oped-cx_pm_0804russia.html#5d45a8dd5f53.
25 Leonid Kuchma, *Ukraina – ne Rossiia* (Moscow, 2003).
26 Mykola Rjabtschuk, *Die reale und die imaginierte Ukraine* (Frankfurt/Main, 2005), p. 71.
27 Ivo Mijnssen, *The Quest for an Ideal Youth in Putin's Russia: Back to Our Future! History, Modernity, and Patriotism According to Nashi, 2005–2013* (Stuttgart, 2014).
28 Gerard Toal, *Near Abroad: Putin, the West, and the Contest over Ukraine and the Caucasus* (Oxford, 2017).
29 Timothy Snyder, 'Ukraine: The War for Truth', lecture at University College London, 25 February 2015, available at: www.youtube.com/watch?v=K8WKuSvTfco.

4 The cultivation of the Habsburg myth in Galicia and Bukovina

In 2009, Arseniy Yatsenyuk (born in 1974), who would later serve as prime minister (2014–2016), commissioned a statue in honour of Emperor Franz Joseph I of Austria (1830–1916) in a small park in his hometown of Chernivtsi (formerly Czernowitz). Yatsenyuk thereby emphasised Ukraine's connection with the Western European tradition, and it was no accident that he selected the famous Austrian Emperor in this context. Franz Joseph reigned for nearly sixty years, from 1848 to 1916. His presence guaranteed that the liberal policy towards nationalities in the Habsburg Empire would remain constant. The sensibility of the Emperor with regard to multi-ethnic problematics is well indicated by the title of his war manifesto, *To My Peoples!*, which he used in 1866 in the Austro-Prussian War and again in 1914 in the First World War. The plural in this title rolled easily off the tongue of Franz Joseph, given that speakers of German made up only about 24 per cent of the population in the dual monarchy; the Emperor knew very well that the Slavic peoples could only be connected to the Habsburg Empire by recognising their rights to cultural autonomy.

Galicia and Bukovina had come under Austrian rule after 1772 (Figure 4.1). The investment made by Vienna in higher learning in the eastern Crown Lands was considerable: Lemberg (Lviv) was granted a university in 1774, and Czernowitz (Chernivtsi) followed in 1875. At first, both universities were German-speaking, but the University of Lemberg was subject to Polonisation after the defeat of Austria in the Austro-Prussian War. So Czernowitz then had at its disposal the only German-speaking university in Austrian Ukraine. One of the first professors at the newly-founded Franz Joseph University in Czernowitz was the Swiss-born philosopher Anton Marty (1847–1914); Joseph Schumpeter (1883–1950), who was later to become a star economist, also occupied his first Chair here, from 1909 to 1911.

In the Habsburg monarchy, the Ukrainians were called 'Ruthenians'. Vienna thereby followed a strategy similar to that of the Tsarist authorities, who spoke merely of 'Little Russians' in order not to allow a 'Ukrainian' nation to be imagined. The Ruthenians enjoyed extensive cultural freedoms in the Habsburg Empire. After Ukrainian-language publications were forbidden in Russian Ukraine in 1863 and 1876, Galicia played an especially important

The Habsburg myth in Galicia and Bukovina 33

Figure 4.1 Ukraine in the nineteenth century

role in Ukrainian literary culture. Reciprocally, the Ruthenians also showed themselves to be grateful subjects; and on account of their loyalty to the Habsburg Emperor, which they proved above all during the revolution of 1848, they became known as the 'Tyroleans of the East'. However, Ukrainian political claims were stirring even in Austrian Galicia. From a Ukrainian point of view, though, it was not the Austrians but rather the Poles who were the main enemies. The poet and publicist Ivan Franko (1856–1916), who wrote his texts in Ukrainian, Polish and German, offers an interesting example. In both 1877 and 1880, he was condemned to several weeks' detention for having allegedly committed popular sedition, and moreover he could not complete his studies at the University of Lemberg. In 1897, Franko wrote a pamphlet with the title *A Poet of Betrayal*, in which he accused the Polish national poet Adam Mickiewicz of avoiding open warfare with his political enemies and of recommending a strategy of hypocrisy. In this essay it is indicative that Franko chose the German language in which to express his view of relations between Ukraine and Poland.

The Marxist theoretician Yulian Bachynsky (1870–1940) also became involved alongside Franko. In 1895, Bachynsky wrote a polemic entitled *Ucraina irredenta* in which he proclaimed that the *ancien régime* in Vienna and St Petersburg would soon meet its end and demanded an independent Ukrainian state with a socialist organisation of its society. Bachynsky was not at all modest in his territorial plans: the new Ukraine should stretch from the River San, a tributary of the Vistula, up to the Caucasus. Inspired by a

Marxist internationalism, Bachynsky used the term 'Ukraine' not in an ethnic sense but rather geographically, so that all inhabitants of this region, whether they were autochthonous, Russian, Polish, Jewish or German, should be integrated into the modern Ukrainian project.

In the internal hierarchy of peoples under the Habsburg monarchy, the position of the Ukrainians was quite low down. From a Viennese point of view, they counted as being less well educated by comparison with the German and Polish populations. This view is clearly reflected in the electoral law of 1907: in order to receive a political mandate, a Ukrainian candidate had to obtain twice as many votes as a Polish competitor. In 1908, a Ukrainian student assassinated the Polish governor in Galicia and thereby protested against the political discrimination that was being shown to his ethnic group; in 1914, Vienna reacted by making concessions, but these measures were not actually implemented because of the advent of war.

After the First World War, Galicia became subject to Polonisation; cultural memories of Austria became limited, in the Second Republic, to its characteristics as an imperialist agent of division. During the Soviet era this narrative was developed further, *mutatis mutandis* – only now, Austria and Poland were counted as oppressors, while it was insisted that the Red Army had brought to the Ukrainians their long-yearned-for freedom.

It is only in quite recent times that a genuine Habsburg renaissance can be observed in Galicia. In 1963, the Italian scholar of German studies Claudio Magris described the Habsburg myth in a path-breaking study,[1] arguing that this myth had replaced concrete historical or social realities with a picturesque fairy-tale world. Magris characterised the myth by means of three elements: (1) the idle postponement of problems, which ultimately was what made the continued existence of the multi-ethnic state possible at all; (2) the apotheosis of the civil service in a rampant bureaucracy that was personified by the 'civil servant in chief' Franz Joseph; and (3) a hedonism, as if in an operetta, that was expressed typically in coffee-house culture.

Ukrainian writers invoke the Austrian past more and more often and thereby reinforce their claim to belong to European cultural heritage, as can be seen most clearly in the case of the so-called 'Stanislav phenomenon'. In the 1980s, in the former Austrian town Stanislau (now Ivano-Frankivsk), an active literary scene took shape to which the leading Western Ukrainian writers of today belonged. Yurii Andrukhovych (born in 1960) wrote an essay in 1994 with the title 'Erz-herz-perz',[2] in which he presented himself, in an ironic way, as a latter-day citizen of the Habsburg monarchy. Andrukhovych emphasised that Stanislav was part of a state to which Venice and Vienna – rather than Tambov and Tashkent – belonged. This state comprised Lombardy and Tuscany as well as Galicia and Transylvania; in order to meet up with Rilke or Klimt, no visa was necessary, one could simply take the relevant train. The literary scholar Stefan Simonek emphasises how Andrukhovych sketches out his nostalgic Habsburg myth against the background of a dismal Soviet reality, thus giving the myth a stronger effect by means of this contrast.[3]

Taras Prokhasko (born in 1968) also repeatedly builds set pieces from Kakanian[4] culture into his prose texts. In 2005, he published a collection of autobiographical fragments under the title *One Could Make Several Stories from This*. Here Prokhasko describes pitiless Soviet realities: his father is arrested; pointless vigils are held at monuments to the Cheka (the secret police); and pupils are harassed by Communist texts.

The return to Austrian authors who came from Ukraine forms another dimension of this updating of the Habsburg myth. In this context, Joseph Roth (1894–1939) is regarded in Galicia as a German-language Ukrainian writer.[5] Roth was born in the Galician *shtetl* Brody. In his works, he frequently mapped out the decline of families that were steeped in tradition and the loss of the 'Imperial and Royal' (*k. und k.*) Habsburg dual monarchy. Yurii Andrukhovych took up this theme in his novel, *Twelve Rings* (2005); he constructs his text as a parody of Roth's novel, *The Radetzky March* (1932).[6] Andrukhovych's protagonist has the same first name as Roth's hero and similarly dies a grotesque death in Galicia as the last representative of his lineage.

As well as Joseph Roth, though, there is a range of other authors from Austrian Galicia who have returned to collective awareness. For instance, Leopold von Sacher-Masoch (1836–1895) spent his childhood in Lemberg as the son of the local Commissioner of the Imperial Police. Some of Sacher-Masoch's stories had already been translated into Ukrainian in the author's lifetime, such as *Don Juan of Kolomyia* and *The Haidamak*, because their plots are set in Galicia. Also famous, however, was Ivan Franko's devastating verdict in a letter from 1891, in which he accused Sacher-Masoch of 'throwing together mendacious and incoherent stuff about Galicia'.[7] Finally, Karl Emil Franzos (1848–1904) became a celebrated author thanks to his collection of novellas, *The Jews of Barnow* (1877). The fictional 'Barnow' refers to Chortkiv, Franzos' Galician hometown. In his novel, *For the Right* (1882), Franzos established a literary memorial to the Carpathian brigand Oleksa Dovbush. Franzos, in two of his essays, was also the first German-language writer to have concerned himself with the Ukrainian national poet, Taras Shevchenko.

Roth, Sacher-Masoch and Franzos are all rooted in Galicia, but in Bukovina too, a renaissance of German-language literature has been going on for some time. The great extent to which Austrian tradition is recognised on an official level as well is shown by the fact that President Yanukovych awarded the Order of Yaroslav the Wise to the former Crown Prince Otto Habsburg (1912–2011) on the occasion of the latter's visit to Czernowitz in 2007. Since 2010, a literature festival with the programmatic title *Meridian* has taken place in Czernowitz. The event thereby alludes to the famous speech that Paul Celan gave in 1960 when he was honoured with the Georg Büchner Prize of the German Academy for Language and Literature. In 'The Meridian', Celan set out the central principles of his writing. He defended above all the 'darkness' of the text, which had to 'alienate' its reader; only in this way could 'the I – as alienated – set itself free'.[8]

The central figure of reference for the literary scene in Czernowitz is the writer Olha Kobylianska (1863–1942), who is regarded today as an important representative of Ukrainian literary modernity. The town promenade, formerly known as Herrengasse ('Lords' Lane'), now bears the name of Kobylianska, and the town theatre is also named after her. As a child, she had written her first poems in Polish; later she published her German-language stories in magazines in Vienna, Berlin and Stuttgart. Around the beginning of the 1890s, Kobylianska eventually switched from German to Ukrainian. In her works she subtly analyses female consciousness as it is torn between bourgeois and same-sex love.

The poet Rose Ausländer (1901–1988) also came from Czernowitz. In the 1920s, she emigrated to New York, but she came back to Europe in 1931. In 1939, she published her first volume of poems, *The Rainbow*. In her poem 'Into Life' (1939), she coined the metaphor of 'black milk' that would feature a few years later at the beginning of Celan's famous 'Death Fugue'. In the winter of 1940 to 1941, she was arrested by the Soviet NKVD and spent several weeks in prison. She worked through her prison experience in a most impressive way in the poem 'In Jail' (1979):

> I was brought
> to the dungeon
> I don't know why
> What are you
> a poet is nothing
> what are you really
> In my cell
> I told the young woman
> fairy tales, poems
> she learnt them easily
> From clay-like bread
> we made chess pieces
> played until eye
> appeared in the spyhole
> Playing forbidden
> Reading and writing forbidden
> Ten minutes in the courtyard
> The sky a
> blue legend
> The cloud beckoned white
> your mother awaits.[9]

As if by a miracle, Ausländer managed to survive the German Occupation. In 1946, she emigrated once again to New York, where she worked as a foreign language secretary – and where, up to 1956, she wrote a series of exquisite poems in English.[10] She spent the final years of her life in Düsseldorf, writing poetry well into old age:

If I despair
I write poems
If I'm cheerful
poems write themselves
in me
Who am I
if I do not
write.[11]

Paul Celan (1920–1970), who by now belongs to the innermost canon of German-language poetry, grew up in Czernowitz in impoverished circumstances. In the multi-ethnic context of Bukovina, he soon mastered not only his native German, but also Romanian, Ukrainian and Yiddish. In 1942, Celan lost his parents, who were Jewish, in a Transnistrian labour camp that had been set up by the Romanian regime, this wartime regime having made a pact with Hitler's Germany. Celan himself also had to carry out forced labour. After the Second World War, Celan escaped from communist Bucharest, via Vienna, to Paris. His love affair with the Austrian writer Ingeborg Bachmann (1926–1973) belongs to this period. Celan took his own life in Paris in 1970.

In his poetry, Celan continued the traditions of German Romanticism, French Symbolism and Russian Acmeism. He established an eminent reputation for himself as a translator of the poetry of Stéphane Mallarmé, Osip Mandelstam and Emily Dickinson; foreign sounds reverberated in his ear, and he characterised his own poems as 'translations without originals'.

With his famous 'Death Fugue' (1945), Celan managed to contradict Theodor Adorno's infamous dictum that it was barbaric to write poems at all after Auschwitz.[12] Celan's poem was first published in 1947 in a Romanian translation with the title 'Death Tango'. The so-called Goll affair then caused quite a stir, some years later: the widow of the poet Ivan Goll accused Celan of having plagiarised her husband's poem 'Chant des invaincus' (1942) in 'Death Fugue'.[13] These allegations, which were proven to be baseless, affected Celan very deeply. In a letter from 1962 he describes the accusations of plagiarism as a 'fulfilment of the Final Solution after the event' in his own person.[14]

A writer who remains less well known than Celan is his second cousin Selma Meerbaum-Eisinger (1924–1942), who also grew up in Czernowitz. Her small but impressive body of work comprises a mere 57 poems. In her 'Poem' (1941), she works through the traumatising experience when SS troops marched into her hometown:

I'd like to live.
I'd like to laugh and to lift heavy loads
and I'd like to fight and love and hate
and I'd like to hold the sky in my hands

and I'd like to be free and to breathe and cry
I don't want to die. No!
No.
Life is red,
Life is mine.
Mine and yours.
Mine.
[...]
The moon is bright silver in the blue.
The poplars are grey.
The wind hurtles me along.
The street is clear.
Then ...
They come then
and choke me.
Me and you
dead.
Life is red,
hurtling and laughing.
Overnight
I am
dead.[15]

Together with her parents, Meerbaum-Eisinger was confined to the newly created ghetto and was later transported to a Transnistrian labour camp; she died there, 18 years old, from epidemic typhus and emaciation.

The fluctuating fortunes of the town of Czernowitz are to some extent imprinted on the biography of the writer Josef Burg (1912–2009). Burg came from Vyzhnytsia (Wischnitz), a small town in Bukovina in which exclusively Yiddish was spoken. As a young man Burg attended the teachers' seminary in Czernowitz, and in 1935 he travelled to Vienna in order to begin a degree in German studies. After the *Anschluss* annexing Austria to Hitler's Germany, though, Burg – as a Jew – was obliged to leave the Austrian capital. He returned to Czernowitz, but even there he soon found himself to be a stranger once again: the pro-fascist regime in Bucharest deprived him of Romanian citizenship. Burg therefore welcomed the Red Army at first when they marched into Czernowitz; he hoped for a more just society, free of anti-Semitism. There was already a tradition of communist engagement in Burg's family, and his brother had fallen as a volunteer in the Spanish Civil War. While the Second World War was still going on, Burg travelled to the Soviet Union and found a position as a German teacher in a Volga German village. The German population, though, because of alleged collaboration with Hitler, was soon deported. Burg worked for almost twenty years in various schools and universities in Russia. It was not until 1959 that he returned to Czernowitz, where certainly no possibilities of publishing his work were available to him, for the Soviet Union had decreed that there was to be no more Yiddish literature in Czernowitz – so Burg and his artistic work were passed over in silence. For a period of forty years Burg could not publish any books. Then in 1980 and 1983, at last, two volumes of Yiddish stories appeared in Moscow that were characterised by their high mastery of style.

The trauma of the Holocaust repeatedly emerges in Burg's texts. A brief two-part composition with the title 'Rigour of the Law' is especially striking in this context: in the first half, Burg starkly describes how a mother and her child are murdered by an SS officer, while in the second half we are shown the murderer years later. Calling an old Jew to him on his deathbed, the murderer asks the Jew for forgiveness; the Jew listens to the confession of the Nazi henchman – and leaves the room without saying a word. In his stories, Burg foregoes complicated courses of action, leaving much that remains open, and suspending the boundary that divides the world of the author from the world of the reader. Attention is thus drawn to a tradition in decline, in which sensuality and wisdom are connected to form a style of writing that has an almost Biblical conciseness.[16]

Josef Burg was one of the last representatives of Yiddish culture in Czernowitz. Today the impressive but decaying Jewish cemetery on a hill on the far bank of the River Prut is one of the few surviving testimonies to the former greatness of this cultural tradition in the 'Little Vienna' of the imperial age.

Notes

1 Claudio Magris, *Der habsburgische Mythos in der österreichischen Literatur* (Salzburg, 1966).
2 Yuri Andrukhovych, *My Final Territory: Selected Essays*, ed. Michael M. Naydan (Toronto, 2018).
3 Stefan Simonek, 'Der Habsburger-Mythos als Moment einer regionalen Identität Galiziens? (Beispiele aus der zeitgenössischen ukrainisch-galizischen Literatur)', *Litteraria Humanitas*, XVI (Brno, 2012) [= Dialogy o slovanských literaturách: tradice a perspektivy], pp. 177–186.
4 This ironic neologism is found in Robert Musil's novel, *The Man Without Qualities*, trans. Sophie Wilkins and Burton Pike (London, 1995), and refers to the phrase *kaiserlich und königlich* ('Imperial and Royal'), used to characterise the Habsburg dual monarchy; the German abbreviation is *k. und k.*, the *k* being pronounced *ka*.
5 Alois Woldan, 'Interkulturelle Beziehungen in den Literaturen Galiziens', in *Germanistische Erfahrungen und Perspektiven der Interkulturalität*, ed. Franciszek Grucza, Hans-Jörg Schwenk and Magdalena Olpińska (Warsaw, 2005), pp. 111–129; Alois Woldan, 'Galizische Topoi als Argumente in der ukrainischen Identitätsdebatte', in *Wo liegt die Ukraine: Standortbestimmung einer europäischen Kultur* (Bausteine zur Slavischen Philologie und Kulturgeschichte Reihe A: Slavistische Forschungen, vol. LXIV), ed. Steffen Höhne and Justus H. Ulbricht (Cologne, 2009), pp. 92–108.
6 Joseph Roth, *The Radetzky March*, trans. Michael Hofmann (London, 2002).
7 Ostap Sereda, 'Leopold fon Zakher Mazokh i ukrains'kyi natsional'nyi rukh u Halychyny u 60-kh rokakh', in *Ukraiina: Kul'turna spadchyna, natsional'na svidomist', derzhavnist'*, Prosphonema (Lviv, 1998), pp. 561–569.

8 Paul Celan, 'The Meridian', in *The Meridian: Final Version – Drafts – Materials*, trans. Pierre Joris (Stanford, CA, 2011), pp. 1–14.
9 Rose Ausländer, *Treffpunkt der Winde: Gedichte 1979* (Frankfurt/Main, 1991), p. 22.
10 Rose Ausländer, *The Forbidden Tree: Englische Gedichte* (Frankfurt/Main, 1995).
11 Rose Ausländer, *Gelassen atmet der Tag: Gedichte* (Frankfurt/Main, 1976), p. 154.
12 Theodor W. Adorno, 'Cultural Criticism and Society', in *Prisms*, trans. Samuel and Shierry Weber (Cambridge, MA, 1981), p. 34; Adorno modifies his dictum in *Negative Dialectics*, trans. E. B. Ashton (London, 1973), pp. 362–363.
13 Jean Bollack, *Dichtung wider Dichtung: Paul Celan und die Literatur* (Göttingen, 2006), p. 53.
14 Markus May, ed., *Celan-Handbuch: Leben, Werk, Wirkung* (Stuttgart, 2012), p. 22.
15 Selma Meerbaum-Eisinger, 'Poem', in Selma Meerbaum-Eisinger, *Ich bin in Sehnsucht eingehüllt: Gedichte eines jüdischen Mädchens an seinen Freund* (Czernowitz, 2012), pp. 62–66.
16 Josef Burg, *Sterne altern nicht: Ausgewählte Erzählungen* (Winsen/Luhe, 2004).

5 Poland as friend and foe
From the Volhynia Massacre to the Polish initiatives for Ukraine in the EU

Today Poland stands as the best advocate on behalf of Ukraine in Europe. Together with Sweden, Poland was decisively involved in bringing about the EU Association Agreement that, after considerable delay, was eventually signed by representatives of the Ukrainian government in 2014. Poland had already played a constructive role during the Orange Revolution of 2004: the Polish President at the time, Aleksander Kwaśniewski (born in 1954), successfully mediated between the factions in the conflict.

There are numerous connections between Poland and Ukraine, not only in politics but also in academia and in the private sector. A great many Ukrainian researchers and students, including those engaged in doctoral studies, contribute to the success of Polish universities and academies. At the same time a considerable part of the work in Polish households is carried out by Ukrainian women, and Ukrainian women are also widely engaged in both childcare and care of the elderly.

The two countries have grown together in terms of transport connections as well. Admittedly, an external Schengen border runs between Ukraine and Poland; nonetheless there are simplifications in place as far as local border traffic is concerned. Numerous connections exist between Poland and Ukraine by means of bus and train, and the network of the Polish airline LOT features five Ukrainian destinations, namely, Kyiv, Lviv, Kharkiv, Zaporizhia and Odessa.

These close relations should not hide the fact that, until quite recently, Poland was traditionally seen in Ukraine as one of its stereotypical enemies. Before the Polish partitions at the end of the eighteenth century, broad areas of Ukraine up to the River Dnieper had belonged to the Polish-Lithuanian Commonwealth. The so-called *Rzeczpospolita* ('Commonwealth') represented the greatest regional power in the eastern Europe of the seventeenth century: Galicia, Volhynia and Podolia all found themselves under Polish rule. Many towns were strongly influenced by the Polish aristocracy, while in the countryside Ukrainian-speaking peasants were predominant. The opposition between Poles and Ukrainians was therefore not just national but also social in nature. Among the educated Ukrainian elite, the phenomenon of social climbing and assimilation was especially widespread. In the sixteenth and seventeenth centuries, the Ukrainian upper class subjected itself to an almost total process of Polonisation. Convincing evidence of this process can be found in the self-designation of the nobleman Stanisław Orzechowski (1513–1566), who described himself as *gente Ruthenus, natione Polonus* ['Ruthenian by origin but Polish by nationality']; this double consciousness of an ethnic Ukrainian who saw himself at the same time as a Polish citizen became a model for the Ukrainian aristocracy in the *Rzeczpospolita*.[1]

The importance of the Church Union of Brest in 1596 for Ukrainian nation-building can hardly be exaggerated. At that time, the Orthodox Ukrainian population on the territory of the *Rzeczpospolita* was united with the Catholic Church. The Orthodox rites survived, but the so-called Greek-Catholic Church recognised the Roman Pope as head of the Church. Even though – or perhaps precisely because – the united congregations were repeatedly oppressed by the Tsarist and Communist authorities in the nineteenth and twentieth centuries, a specifically Ukrainian confessional identity developed into an important pillar of Ukrainian national awareness.

Poland had taken possession of Ukraine not only in territorial but also in cultural terms. This hegemony even continued after the end of Polish statehood which was sealed by Prussia, Austria and Russia, the partitioning powers, in 1795. In the nineteenth century, Poland lived on not as a state but in terms of an often over-inflated national culture. In Romantic literature, a prominent 'Ukrainian School' was formed, represented above all by Antoni Malczewski (1793–1826), Seweryn Goszczyński (1801–1876) and Józef Bohdan Zaleski (1802–1886). All three poets came from the south-eastern territory of the now defunct *Rzeczpospolita* that was thought of as 'Polish Ukraine'. In 1825, Malczewski had published a long poem with the title *Maria: A Ukrainian Story in Verse* that, with its tragic plot, stood firmly in the tradition of dark Romanticism: a demonic father sends his son and his brother-in-law to war against the Tartars, in order to murder his unloved daughter-in-law Maria.

Goszczyński then wanted to tie in with the success of Malczewski's literary shaping of Ukraine, and so he wrote the poem *The Castle of Kaniów* (1828). He summarised the content of his poem in a self-mocking letter:

> Seduction of a virgin, revenge, all murders imaginable, a Polish nobleman who commits tyrannical crimes, a nightingale that prophesies death, an executioner, two insane women, a gang that kills Poles, another gang that kills the murderers, torrents of blood, devilish hordes, and so on.[2]

Zaleski, finally, transposed the genre of the *duma*, the philosophical poem, into Polish literature and wrote *The Duma about Wacław* (1819) and *The Dumka of Hetman Kosiński* (1822). He drew a sentimental and idyllic picture of Ukraine, which seemed to him as if it were the Garden of Eden before the Fall, and in his representation of the history shared by Ukrainians and Poles, the wish was father to the thought. Zaleski extolled a utopian alliance between the Ukrainian Cossacks and the Poles, who together were to protect the south-eastern border of the Christian *Rzeczpospolita* from the Turks. Many Poles from Ukraine identified with such a harmonious idea: while they understood themselves to be Polish patriots, they were also closely connected to Ukraine and to the Ukrainian population.

Perhaps the most popular image of Ukraine in Polish culture derives from the best-selling author Henryk Sienkiewicz (1846–1916), who, in 1905, was honoured with the Nobel Prize in Literature. His trilogy was avidly devoured by generations of young readers; in these three historical novels, namely, *With Fire and Sword* (1884), *The Deluge* (1886) and *Fire in the Steppe* (1888), he painted a colourful picture of Polish Ukraine in the seventeenth century as an epoch. For Sienkiewicz, though, it was not a question of making an accurate reappraisal of historical events, but rather of strengthening Polish national sentiment. He therefore differentiated in a one-dimensional way between the 'good Poles' and the 'bad Ukrainians'. Moreover, several critics suspected that Sienkiewicz relied on his experiences as a journalist in the American West, from 1876 to 1878, when he came to describe the Ukrainian steppe.

Austrian Galicia in the nineteenth century was an important laboratory for exploring how Poles and Ukrainians might coexist. During the revolutions of 1848, both Polish and Ukrainian aspirations to autonomy made themselves felt. On the Ukrainian side, ultimately, these aspirations culminated in the demand for Galicia to be divided up into a Polish West and a Ukrainian East, whereas the Poles wanted to hold on to the status quo of a Galicia dominated by Poland.

Furthermore, Galicia also remained the most prominent stage for the confrontation between Poles and Ukrainians. After the collapse of the Habsburg Empire, events escalated, and in the winter of 1918 to 1919, the street fighting that had set Ukrainians against Poles was transformed into an outright war. The defence of Lemberg by Polish schoolchildren and students has now become one of the most important national myths in Poland; the so-called 'Young Eagles of Lemberg' or 'Lwów Eaglets' (*Orlęta Lwowskie*) held the town until military reinforcements could arrive. The young Polish defenders of the town who died during the siege were commemorated by a monumental tomb, in the Lychakiv Cemetery of Lemberg, which then fell into disrepair during the Soviet period. In the 1990s, a fierce dispute ensued concerning the reconstruction of the tomb dedicated to the 'Eagles of Lemberg', since Ukrainian nationalists saw in it a symbol of the oppression of Ukrainians by the Poles. The dispute could not be settled until 2005, after the Orange Revolution had been supported unconditionally by Poland.

The conflict over Lemberg in 1918 was a dramatic prelude that overshadowed all the later coalitions between Poland and Ukraine. In 1920, the leaders of the newly founded Second Polish Republic and of the Ukrainian People's Republic, Józef Piłsudski (1867–1935) and Symon Petliura (1879–1926) respectively, signed a mutual assistance pact that was directed against Bolshevist Russia. The war of aggression waged by Poland and Ukraine seemed at first to meet with success: in

May 1920, the Polish forces took Kyiv, but after a mere three weeks they were driven out again. The Red Army pursued Piłsudski right up to the gates of Warsaw – but in a dramatic and decisive battle, the Poles were able to ward off the Soviet attack at the last minute.

The British diplomat Edgar Vincent, Viscount D'Abernon (1857–1941), counted this engagement among the eighteen most important battles of world history, putting it on the same level as the victory of the Athenians at Marathon, the Norman conquest of England at Hastings and Napoleon's defeat at Waterloo.[3] In Polish historiography, the Battle of Warsaw is often described as the 'Miracle at the Vistula'. Given such mythical exaggerations, it is hardly surprising that Polish popular culture has by now also become aware of this subject matter. In September 2011, the monumental film *Battle of Warsaw 1920* made its debut in 298 Polish cinemas; the first Polish feature film to be made in 3D, it broke all records. With a budget of US$8 million and an array of over 3,500 extras, *Battle of Warsaw, 1920* was one of the most lavish productions in the entire history of Polish cinema. The director, Jerzy Hoffman (born in 1932), had already brought Henryk Sienkiewicz's trilogy to the cinema screen in a series of very popular films. In the Communist Polish People's Republic, the Polish victory over the Red Army was of course not permitted as an artistic theme. By now, though, the ideological auspices had radically changed. The 'only authentic Polish victory', according to Hoffman, 'saved at least an important part of Europe, if not the whole of Europe, from Bolshevism'.[4]

Hoffman is, however, not only a Polish patriot but also a friend of Ukraine: in *Battle of Warsaw, 1920* it is shown in detail how the Cossacks fight side by side with the Poles against the Bolshevist usurpers, and in the film Józef Piłsudski claims that he wants to grant Kyiv to the Ukrainians once it has been conquered by the Poles. Already in 2007, Hoffman had filmed the highly Ukrainophile documentary, *Ukraine: The Birth of a Nation*. Hoffman, who is married to a woman from Kyiv, divided his film into four episodes: 'From Rus' to Ukraine', 'Ukraine or Little Russia?', 'Together Forever' and 'Independence'. These titles alone indicate that, above all, Hoffman is producing an anti-Russian representation of the events in question. Seeing Russia as the common enemy, whether in the form of the Tsarist Empire or the Soviet regime, offers the most reliable foundation for a close alliance between Poland and Ukraine.

The inter-war years, though, did not offer much ground for optimism. In the Second Polish Republic there was a nationalistic consensus that transcended all party divisions; the new state had to be as ethnically homogeneous as possible. The Ukrainian minority in Galicia was thus supposed to be subjected to Polonisation. As far as the Jews were concerned, even liberally inclined intellectuals such as Jerzy Giedroyc (1906–2000) considered coercive economic measures and forced expatriation to Madagascar. After the May Coup of 1926, an authoritarian regime was installed in Poland that merely maintained a façade of democracy. Among the ranks of the Ukrainian nationalists, forms of terrorist aggression arose: in 1926, the Lviv school superintendent Stanisław Sobiński was murdered, and in 1928 and 1929 this was followed by bombings aimed at the editorial office of the newspaper *Słowo Polskie* and at the exhibitions of the Eastern Trade Fair (*Targi Wschodnie*). At the beginning of the 1930s, the number of attacks and acts of sabotage increased, to the point where the government ultimately proceeded to carry out a policy of so-called pacification: the Polish police acted like an occupying power in the Eastern Voivodeships of the country, systematically violating the constitutional rights to freedom of the Ukrainian citizens of Poland. Admittedly, terrorist attacks were curtailed to a certain extent by this policy – but at the high price of a further alienation between Poles and Ukrainians. Isolated attacks continued to cause a stir, moreover; and, in 1934, Bronisław Pieracki, the Polish Minister of Internal Affairs who was given the nickname 'Bronito Pieratini' because of his sympathies for Italian fascism, was murdered by a Ukrainian nationalist. The famous leader of the extremist Organisation of Ukrainian Nationalists (OUN) in Galicia, Stepan Bandera (1909–1959), was charged with complicity in this murder and sentenced to death. The verdict was eventually commuted to life imprisonment, and Bandera spent the years from 1934 to 1939 in the prison of Wronki in Western Poland.

The attempt to subject Ukraine to Polonisation was also reflected in official statistics. In 1931, the census produced the following result for Galicia: 2,246,000 Poles, 1,665,000 Ukrainians and 1,119,000 Ruthenians.[5] By means of artificially dividing up the Ukrainians into two ethnic groups, the impression was thus created that the Poles represented the numerically strongest ethnicity in Galicia.

Polish attempts at rapprochement with the Ukrainians, such as the so-called 'Volhynia Experiment', remained the exception and not the rule. Henryk Józewski (1892–1981), who had grown up in Kyiv, actively promoted the development of Ukrainian culture when he was the Voivode (Governor) of Volhynia in the 1930s. He thereby wanted to create an 'enclave of 1920 ideology', similar to when Piłsudski and Petliura had fought together against Soviet Russia. There is a bitter irony of fate here: it was the very same Volhynia that became the scene, a few years later, of the bloodiest confrontation between Poles and Ukrainians.

The German invasion of Galicia had been welcomed to a great extent by the Ukrainian population; Hitler had attacked Poland as well as Soviet Russia, and he therefore appeared to many Ukrainians as a natural ally. In 1939, Stepan Bandera had become the leader of the 'Organisation of Ukrainian Nationalists' (OUN). The OUN and its military wing, the Ukrainian Insurgent Army (UPA), at first collaborated with the German invaders. In 1942, many Ukrainian soldiers participated in mass murders of the Jewish population of Ukraine. UPA members could apply what they had learnt from this experience of murder a year later, when they killed around 50,000 Poles, among them many women and children, in Volhynia. In 1944 and 1945,

Polish partisans took revenge for this massacre by murdering Ukrainian families in the region of Chełm.

After the Second World War, the opposition between Poles and Ukrainians remained. In 'Operation Vistula' (1947), Ukrainians and Lemkos were forcibly relocated within Poland. Even after the official end of the war, the UPA continued to fight in Galicia until the early 1950s. The Polish Communist Government therefore deported the Ukrainian population from border areas, settling them instead in the new – formerly German – western areas. In this process, attention was paid to ensuring Polish dominance in the new settlements, so that the Ukrainian section of the population would nowhere exceed 10 per cent. The declared aim of Operation Vistula consisted in the assimilation of the Ukrainians into the Polish national culture; in this way the 'Ukrainian question' in Poland was to be solved once and for all.

Paradoxically, the Communist Polish People's Republic, which itself claimed credit for having overcome bourgeois nationalism, was in fact ethnically a lot more homogeneous than the Second Polish Republic had been before the war. Because of the Holocaust, forced migrations, and realignments of territory, 95 per cent of the population were now Polish Catholics, who showed little sympathy for minorities. In a study carried out in 2001, positive views of Ukraine were expressed by only 12 per cent of the Poles who were surveyed; and on a scale formed by 28 nations, the Ukrainians were assigned the fourth-from-last place – thus being even more unpopular than the Russians.[6]

Again, in 2003, which saw the sixtieth anniversary of the massacre in Volhynia, the rifts in historical memory between Poland and Ukraine clearly came to light. In Poland, there was disappointment that the Ukrainian President Leonid Kuchma had not apologised for the Ukrainian atrocities, whereas in Ukraine there was a sense that Poland should be reminded of its partial responsibility for what happened, based on the political suppression suffered by the Ukrainians in the Second Polish Republic. In 2011, the Ukrainian historian Volodymyr Viatrovych (born in 1977) published a book that presents the events in Volhynia as a continuation of the Polish-Ukrainian war of 1918–1919. The title of the book is already a provocation: *The Second Polish-Ukrainian War*.[7] Viatrovych has this war begin in 1942 and end in 1947. This bold contextualisation has the advantage that, in a 'war', violence naturally occurs on both sides. He explains the massacre in Volhynia as a spontaneous aggression on the part of Ukrainian peasants against the Poles who had suppressed them for such a long time.[8] From 2014 to 2019, Viatrovych headed the Ukrainian National Institute of Remembrance.

In July 2016, the Polish parliament passed a bill that qualified the events in Volhynia in 1943 as a genocide against the Polish people. In October 2016, Wojciech Smarzowski presented the feature film *Volhynia* (also known in English as *Hatred*) that depicts the massacre in the cruellest possible terms. The film shows atrocities like the beheading of a Polish mother, the burning of a child in a sheaf, the tearing apart of the body of a Polish officer by two horses, and the evisceration of a living victim. The Polish and Ukrainian reactions to this emotional and dramatic film took opposite stances. Leading Polish newspapers acclaimed the film and praised Smarzowski as a new Renaissance painter who had found an aesthetic for the depiction of evil, while Ukrainian intellectuals were disappointed and held that *Volhynia* was a 'school of hatred'.[9]

The debates over the film *Volhynia* endangered the reconciliation between Ukrainians and Poles that had occurred during the Orange Revolution in 2004. This was when the Polish commitment to a European Ukraine became clear for the first time, a commitment that was also strongly manifested in 2014, the year of crisis.

The Polish Government was able to find support for a new conception of Ukraine in the preliminary work done by the editors of the influential *émigré* magazine *Kultura*, which first appeared briefly in Rome and then in Paris from 1947 to 2000. *Kultura* – in stark contrast to the conservative Polish *émigré* milieu in London – advocated the recognition of post-war boundaries: Ukraine should be strengthened in its relation to Russia, and the Polish claim to Lviv therefore had to be abandoned. Jerzy Giedroyc, the perspicacious editor of *Kultura*, demanded that the post-war period should turn away from the fatal policy with regard to nationalities that had been pursued by the Second Polish Republic. Bohdan Osadchuk (1920–2011), one of the most important advocates of reconciliation between Ukraine and Poland, thought that today, without the work of mediation carried out by *Kultura*, the border area between the two countries could have turned into a 'Polish-Ukrainian Kosovo – a place of mutual murder'.[10] Osadchuk personally attempted to convince Ukrainian politicians that the only route to the West led through Poland. As a model for this reconciliation between the Poles and the Ukrainians, Osadchuk pointed to the friendship between the Germans and the French: today the German-French rapport has become one of the most important supports for the process of European unification, but it was not until near the end of the twentieth century, after long and bitter hostilities, that this rapport was formed.

Notes

1 Serhii Plokhy, *The Origins of Slavic Nations: Premodern Identities in Russia, Ukraine and Belarus* (Cambridge, MA, 2006), p. 169.
2 Maria Janion, *Romantyzm i jego media* (Kraków, 2001), p. 544.
3 Edgar Vincent D'Abernon, *The Eighteenth Decisive Battle of the World: Warsaw, 1920* (London, 1931).
4 Joanna Lenartowicz, '*Battle of Warsaw, 1920*: Interview with Director Jerzy Hoffman', 19 September 2011, available at: http://culture.pl/en/article/battle-of-wa rsaw-1920-interview-with-director-jerzy-hoffman.
5 Volodymyr Kubijovyc, *Les régions occidentales de l'Ukraine sous l'administration polonaise (1919–1939)* (Paris, 1966), p. 11.
6 Kai-Olaf Lang, 'Polen und die Ukraine: Eine strategische Partnerschaft für das neue Europa?', in *Die Ukraine, Polen und Europa: Europäische Identität an der EU-Ostgrenze*, ed. Renata Makarska and Basil Kerski (Osnabrück, 2004), pp. 29–54.

7 Volodymyr Viatrovych, *Druha pol'sko-ukrains'ka viina, 1942–1947* (Kyiv, 2011).
8 Andrei Portnov, 'Istorii dlia domashnego upotrebleniia', *Ab Imperio*, III (2012), pp. 309–338.
9 Ulrich Schmid, 'Polnische Opfergeschichten: Die Filme *Miasto 44, Smoleńsk* und *Wołyń*', *Osteuropa*, XI–XII (2016), pp. 135–148.
10 Bohdan Osadczuk, 'Jerzy Giedroyc und die polnisch-ukrainischen Beziehungen', in *Die Ukraine, Polen und Europa: Europäische Identität an der EU-Ostgrenze*, ed. Renata Makarska and Basil Kerski (Osnabrück, 2004), pp. 177–187.

6 National independence and regional differences

After 1991, Ukraine became an independent state for the first time in its history (apart from the brief intermezzo of the 'Ukrainian People's Republic' after the First World War). The degree of loyalty to the new state, though, varied greatly in the different regions. After the collapse of the Soviet Union, Ukraine adopted the borders of the Ukrainian Soviet Socialist Republic, which in this form had only existed since 1954. In the course of the Second World War, numerous territories from other states were incorporated into Ukraine (Figure 6.1): Poland relinquished Galicia, including Lwów; Czechoslovakia lost Transcarpathia, including Uzhhorod; and Romania had to give up North Bukovina, including Czernowitz, as well as the territory of Izmail.

Galicia has always been considered the cradle of Ukrainian nationalism. Many Galicians regard their own region as a kind of Ukrainian 'Piedmont';

Figure 6.1 The regions of Ukraine

from this point of view, the rest of Ukraine is supposed to catch up with that level of national consciousness which is already present in Galicia. To its inhabitants, Galicia counts as the centre of Ukrainian national culture. As a result, the Galician population, in comparison to the whole of Ukraine, is also inclined to be much more intolerant with regard to all other nations. This is the case for Russia above all, which is strongly rejected, but also for Jews, Poles and Romanians. However, this pronounced Ukrainian national consciousness has itself also led to frustrations, and today many Galicians feel like the 'stepchildren' of their own nation. In a study carried out in 2003, a third of the people consulted who were from Lviv advocated an autonomous Galician state if Ukraine were to join the Union of Belarus and Russia.[1] Such a wish could of course find support in historical experience as well: in 1918 and 1919, a 'West Ukrainian People's Republic' existed in Galicia whose unification with the rest of Ukraine ultimately failed as a result of Petliura's pact with Poland. The crisis in Donbas has also given a boost to those voices in Galicia who have been calling for the contested territories in the East to be given up, arguing that people in Donbas still remain rooted in Soviet mentalities and thus should not be integrated into the project of a modern Ukrainian nation state.[2]

There is a strong regional self-awareness in Transcarpathia too. Already in 1989, a movement of separatists was formed there, basing their claims on the alleged existence of a distinct Carpatho-Rusyn people. One of the most famous defenders of this position is Paul Robert Magocsi, a historian at the University of Toronto. Magocsi considers that, since 1848, the Rusyns have constructed a national identity of their own.[3] This process has been facilitated by Transcarpathia's frequent changes of nationality. The region first belonged to the Hungarian half of the dual monarchy forming the Habsburg Empire; while during the inter-war years, Transcarpathia was part of the single functioning democracy in Eastern Europe, namely, Masaryk's Czechoslovakia. The Germans and the Slovaks dominated the discourse about national minorities in Czechoslovakia, though, so that the Rusyns rarely managed to draw attention to themselves. The national aspirations of the Rusyns nonetheless outlasted this inter-war period. In May 1944, a group of priests from Transcarpathia wrote a letter to Stalin. They asked the dictator to set up a separate Carpatho-Rusyn Soviet Republic.[4] Nothing came of this plan, of course, but it is indicative in its anti-Ukrainian impetus. Today Rusyns would emphasise that they are recognised as a national minority in seven Central European states. In the official language rules established by Kyiv, the Rusyns represent a Ukrainian 'sub-ethnicity'. Be that as it may, the Rusyns themselves today mostly see as their main rivals not the Ukrainians but rather the Galicians; and in Transcarpathia, warnings are therefore often made about a 'Galician expansion'.[5]

The Ukrainians of Bukovina have also cultivated a specific identity against the background of their eventful history. Until 1775, Bukovina was under the sovereignty of the Ottoman Empire, and thus it was not affected by the

Church Union of Brest in 1596. The Ruthenians in Bukovina remained Orthodox, and thereby – unlike the Galicians – they did not possess a confessional identity of their own that could become the germ cell for a Ukrainian national awareness. Under Austrian rule a strong convergence with German culture took place. The University of Czernowitz was founded in 1875, in order to satisfy the educational needs of the German-speaking elite and of the assimilated Ruthenians. It was only gradually that Ukrainian forums such as *Ruska Besida* emerged that pursued a separate national project. At the same time, during this period there was fierce rivalry between Ruthenians and Romanians. When in 1921, Bukovina became part of the Kingdom of Romania, not much breathing space was left for Ruthenian culture. Until 1936, every government employee had to give evidence of language skills, and in 1926 the teaching of Ukrainian in schools was forbidden. From the perspective of the Romanian authorities, the Ruthenians in Bukovina were in fact Romanians who had forgotten their own native tongue and thus had to be led back to their ethnic origins once more. Today Bukovina is a Ukrainian region with no claims to autonomy of its own but with a rich multi-cultural past influenced by German, Romanian and Jewish traditions. One example of how these cultures intersect with each other is given by the famous tenor Josef Schmidt (1904–1942), from Czernowitz, who died in the Second World War in the Girenbad internment camp, in the Swiss Canton of Zurich, because of a lack of medical care. Schmidt came from a Jewish family that still felt it belonged to German culture. From 1925 to 1926, Schmidt received his vocal training at the Academy of Music in Berlin, and then he completed his military service in Romania in 1927. After the Nazis seized power, Schmidt moved to Vienna, but then after the *Anschluss* of Austria in 1938, he had to flee again – first to Belgium, then to the South of France and finally to Switzerland.

The conditions found in Donbas are rather different. In contrast to Galicia or Transcarpathia, there is no regional identity here that could be described in positive terms or that could draw support from a particular cultural development. In the Soviet period, Donbas was taken to be an exemplary region in which the successes of industrialisation were shown in the clearest way; and this prominent position made itself felt in the consciousness of the population of Donbas. After the collapse of the Soviet Union, the numbers of those who simply wanted to consider themselves 'inhabitants of Donbas' were higher than the numbers of those who designated themselves 'Ukrainians' or 'Russians'.[6] To this day, it is above all older people who prefer not to define themselves in national but rather in social or cultural categories: as a pensioner, as a Soviet person or as a mother, for example. Donbas does not distance itself so much from Galicia as it does from the region of Dnipro. The rivalry between Donetsk and Dnipro has significantly intensified in the last twenty years, since the oligarchical clans of each city have been striving to strengthen their own influence at the expense of the other. Before the separatist war, the strongman in Donetsk was Rinat Akhmetov (born in 1966). He controlled a large part of the steel and coal industries in Eastern Ukraine, and possessed considerable political influence as well. In Dnipro, the billionaire Ihor Kolomoyskyi (born in 1963) served for a year as Governor, starting in March 2014. Kolomoyskyi managed to protect his region from separatist influences; and he enjoyed great respect among the local population because he paid the salaries of civil servants and soldiers in Dnipro out of his own personal fortune. However, in 2015, Kolomoyskyi lost out in a personal rivalry that had set him against President Poroshenko. Eventually he retired from politics and chose to spend most of his time abroad. After the inauguration of President Volodymyr Zelensky, Kolomoyskyi returned to Ukraine and resumed exerting his influence.

During the entire twentieth century, Donbas was distinguished by an anti-centralising spirit that was directed, to equal degrees, both against Moscow and against Kyiv. With his 'Party of Regions', Viktor Yanukovych was a typical product of Donbas. One important reason for Yanukovych's failure lies in the loss of the basis for his legitimacy: he had only just taken power in Kyiv, as President, when already he began to be perceived in Donbas as a representative of the hated central powers.

The most complex case among the Ukrainian regions is that of Crimea. In 1954, Crimea was severed from the Russian Soviet Republic and allocated to Ukraine. As the dramatic events of Spring 2014 showed, interpretations of this act in Ukraine and in Russia differ enormously. Putin, in his magisterial speech given in the Duma on 18 March 2014, claimed that Nikita Khrushchev (1894–1971) had 'gifted' Crimea to Ukraine 'in a piece of trickery in a hallway'.[7] The Russian President therefore saw himself justified in speaking of a 'reunification' of Crimea with Russia. In doing so, he was following the usual logic underlying such territorial claims: because of an unjust act, a historic mistake has been made, and so now the original state of affairs is to be restored once more. According to Putin, 'literally everything' on the peninsula was permeated with 'a history in common'. Here Prince Vladimir the Great had been converted to Christianity in 988; here were located the graves of those brave soldiers who in 1783 had brought Crimea 'under Russian rule'; and here the fatherland had been defended in the Crimean War (1853–1856) and in the Second World War. The lengthy array of these arguments is as impressive as it is one-sided. Putin played down the presence on the peninsula of the Greeks, the Scythians, the Sarmatians and the Tatars, and in a later speech even called Crimea a sacred place that, for the Russians, was roughly as important as the Temple Mount is for the Jews.

Beyond the patriotic pathos of Putin, the transferral of Crimea to Ukraine in 1954 looks much more prosaic; it was nothing more and nothing less than a card to be played in a power game concerning the succession to Stalin. Khrushchev had climbed steeply up the career ladder, under Stalin, in the party organisation in Moscow and in Ukraine. When the distrusting dictator died, on 5 March 1953, it was not settled who would succeed him. At first it looked as if Stalin's unscrupulous chief of intelligence, Lavrenti Beria (1899–1953), would take power. After Stalin's death, Beria had immediately become the Minister of Internal Affairs, and he thus had forces of his own at his disposal. At this point

Khrushchev stood in fifth place in the Soviet hierarchy of power, and Beria did not even perceive him to be a serious rival. However, in this situation the arrogant Beria made the same mistake as Trotsky after the death of Lenin: he overestimated his own authority, set out his own position without taking account of other views, and imagined up until the end that he would be safe. Beria, who was from Georgia, clearly distanced himself in Spring 1953 from Stalin's Russophilia and wanted to set his own priorities in Soviet policy concerning ethnic minorities; he thus criticised the dominance of Russian in the areas of Belarus, Lithuania, Estonia and Western Ukraine that had been newly conquered by the Red Army. Beria was even prepared to abandon the German Democratic Republic and, in exchange for an appropriate compensation, to consent to a neutral unified German state. For Khrushchev, the staunch Communist, this was too much to bear; so he waited for a propitious moment – when the commander of the forces of the Ministry of Internal Affairs was not in Moscow because of a military exercise – and had Beria arrested. Only after the execution of his rival, in December 1953, did it become clear that Khrushchev was claiming the Soviet leadership position for himself alone.

The transferral of Crimea to Ukraine appears against this background as a strategic chess move. Khrushchev had grown up in Donetsk, but he always designated himself as a Russian and did not speak any Ukrainian. His own career, though, depended on the loyalty of Ukraine to the Kremlin. During the Second World War, Khrushchev had already worked towards enlarging the territory of Soviet Ukraine, in order to show that the Bolsheviks were looking after the interests of Ukraine better than the Ukrainian nationalists; he was responsible for the westward expansion of Ukraine, and he wanted to allocate the Polish region of Chełm to Ukraine as well. In 1944, Khrushchev had already suggested that Crimea be handed over to Ukraine, because the Crimean Tatars who had been expelled were supposed to be replaced by Ukrainian peasants.

1954 was a special year for relations between Ukraine and Russia: the 300th anniversary of the brotherhood between the two peoples was celebrated. In 1654, the Ukrainian Cossacks had sworn an oath of loyalty to the Russian Tsar in Pereyaslav, in order to gain a powerful ally in the fight against Polish supremacy. From the Russian viewpoint, this treaty is interpreted to this day as showing the will of Ukraine to belong to Russia. In 1954, the official documents referred to the belief that the transfer of Crimea to Ukraine testified to 'the unlimited trust of the great Russian people in the Ukrainian people'. In any case, the transfer of Crimea drew Ukraine closer to the central power in Moscow.[8]

Khrushchev was definitely pursuing an ideological goal in his policies concerning Crimea. He firmly believed that Soviet patriotism – in other words, a civic identity that was based not on a national but rather on a socialist conviction – would in the future render obsolete all the old ethnic distinctions. In public, he therefore justified the territorial transfer of Crimea with practical considerations such as 'economic unity', 'territorial proximity' and the 'close cultural connections' between Crimea and Ukraine. This logic was confirmed by means of infrastructure projects such as the important canal that was built after 1954, for example, and that to this day brings badly needed water for agriculture from the Dnieper to the peninsula.

Historical legitimations of territorial claims, such as those made by Putin in his speech, are easy to refute. In the case of Crimea, it is only necessary to move a little along the axis of time in order to see that belonging to Russia, in the twentieth century, was merely one option among others. After the October Revolution, the Crimean Tatars attempted at first to found a republic of their own. In 1918 and 1919, in the Russian civil war, Crimea was transferred twice between the 'Reds' and the 'Whites'. In this context, the short-lived Soviet republics in Crimea were in each case autonomous entities, whereas the 'White' generals regarded Crimea as an exemplary state in a future Russian federation and as a starting point for the military reconquest of Russia. After the final victory of the Bolsheviks, an autonomous Soviet Socialist Republic was established in Crimea in 1921, which for its part belonged to the Russian Soviet Federative Socialist Republic (the RSFSR), which would later become the dominant republic in the Soviet Union. After the German Occupation in the Second World War, Crimea lost its status as a republic and, for the remainder of the Soviet period, was downgraded to the status of a province. Towards the end of the 1980s, the Crimean Tatars returned from their exile in Uzbekistan to their ancestral areas, and thereby aroused an awareness of the particular status of Crimea among the Russian population as well. During Perestroika, the protests against a planned atomic power station in Crimea were also important: resistance to the decision that had been made unilaterally in Moscow united the inhabitants of Crimea of all nationalities. This helps to explain why a referendum that was held on 20 January 1991, and approved by 93 per cent of all inhabitants of Crimea, demanded the establishment of an autonomous republic as a direct federal subject of the Soviet Union – that is, without belonging to the RSFSR. A few months later, though, the Soviet flag on the roof of the Kremlin was taken down. In 1992, Crimea had already adopted a constitution that envisaged, first of all, statehood, but then – as a result of pressure from the Government in Kyiv – integration into the new Ukrainian state. In a survey in January 2013, thus prior to the Euromaidan protests, only around 10 per cent of inhabitants of Crimea answered the question 'What is your homeland?' by saying 'Russia'; 35 per cent said 'Ukraine'; and over 50 per cent referred to their 'own region', in other words Crimea, as their homeland.[9]

Ukraine is thus a highly heterogeneous state with a distinctive regionalism. One should not conclude from this, however, that Ukraine is incapable of surviving as a state. A range of Western European states possess structures that are at least as heterogeneous, and where separatist tendencies are much more virulent than is the case in Ukraine: prominent examples here would be Flanders in Belgium, Scotland in Great Britain or Catalonia in Spain. Switzerland also belongs to this group of states who must constantly take care to achieve a balance between their regions.

In its constitution of 1996, Ukraine attempted to take account of the problematics of the various regions. In programmatic terms, Article 2 maintains: 'Ukraine is a unitary state'. The decisive pronouncements about regionalism are found in Article 132:

> The territorial configuration of Ukraine is based on the principles of the unity and integrity of its national territory, of the connection between centralisation and decentralisation in the exercise of state power, of well-balanced particularities in terms of history, economy, geography and demography, and of the socio-economic development of the regions with consideration for different ethnic and cultural traditions.

The formulation here about the 'connection between centralisation and decentralisation', which seems almost dialectical, represents the Ukrainian solution to the question of how to achieve a balance between the regions.

Interestingly enough, the way in which the chapters of the currently valid constitution are structured already contradicts the dogma of the unitary Ukrainian state. The whole of Chapter 10 of the Constitution is devoted to the 'Autonomous Republic of Crimea'. Today, though, this problem has receded into the background: the Parliament in Kyiv decided, after the annexation of Crimea, to grant complete autonomy in budgetary matters to the Autonomous Republic. By means of this chess move, dictated by necessity, it was possible to maintain a territorial claim on Crimea without at the same time being vulnerable to the objection that no funds were flowing into this part of Ukrainian national territory.

The slogan of 'federalisation' already made its appearance in 1991 in political debates in Ukraine. Federalism, though, always remained the programme of the opposition. The civil rights movement *Rukh*, for instance, thus promoted the idea of a federal structure for Ukraine in the 1990s, as did Yanukovych's 'Party of Regions' in the early years of the twenty-first century. Every political force that achieved power in Kyiv, however, very quickly disavowed federalism and stood for a unitary Ukrainian state instead. The reason for this is naturally that successive governments did not want to curtail their own authority to govern.

Federalism in Ukraine has no historical tradition at its disposal. In contrast to Switzerland, Germany or the USA, the individual regions in Ukraine have barely managed to obtain a state form of their own. The few exceptions to this are the transitory state experiments that took place shortly after the First World War: in Galicia, the 'West Ukrainian People's Republic' arose, in Donetsk-Krivoy Rog, a Soviet Republic was declared, and, in Crimea, there was an alternation between various state formations. These ephemeral constructions, though, did not establish either a political awareness or a separate tradition of state governance. The federalisation of Ukraine in the contemporary situation today would therefore probably not lead to a regional diversification of political culture, but would rather merely complicate the administrative procedures; and of course the project of federalisation has also been compromised in the eyes of many Ukrainians, because it represents one of the central demands made on Kyiv by Russia in the Minsk agreements in September 2014.

However, since 2014, many decentralising reforms have been introduced by the Ukrainian government. These measures range from the empowerment of local self-government over the amalgamation of administrative entities to improvements in healthcare services.[10] A special role is played by the newly established *hromadas*, which will replace the old local councils that had very few responsibilities. The formation of *hromadas* is strongly incentivised, since these new entities should receive much more money from the central government and are given more powers. This process is very popular among Ukrainian citizens in all regions.[11]

Notes

1 Mykola Rjabchuk, *Dvi Ukraini* (Kyiv, 2003), p. 209.
2 Andrii Portnov, 'Ukraina i ee "dal'nii" i "blizhnii" vostok', 31 July 2014, available at: http://urokiistorii.ru/blogs/andrei-portnov/52153.
3 Paul Robert Magocsi, *The Shaping of a National Identity: Subcarpathian Rus', 1848–1948* (Cambridge, MA, 1978).
4 Leonid Kuchma, *Ukraina – ne Rossiia* (Moscow, 2003), p. 53.
5 Andrej Mal'gin, *Ukraina – sobornost' i regionalizm* (Simferopol', 2005), p. 165.
6 Yurii Savel'ev, 'Konflikt subkul'tur v sovremennoj Ukraine ne etnicheskoi prirody', in *Dialog ukrainskoi i russkoi kul'tur: Materialy mezhdunarodnoi koferencii* (Kyiv, 1997), p. 224.
7 Address by President of the Russian Federation, 18 March 2014, available at: http://en.kremlin.ru/events/president/news/20603. The official English translation is somewhat softer than the Russian original: 'The decision was made behind the scenes.'
8 Gwendolyn Sasse, *The Crimea Question: Identity, Transition, and Conflict* (Cambridge, MA, 2007), pp. 107–126.
9 Grigore Pop-Eleches and Graeme Robertson, 'Do Crimeans Actually Want to Join Russia?', *Washington Post*, 6 March 2014, available at: www.washingtonpost.com/news/monkey-cage/wp/2014/03/06/do-crimeans-actually-want-to-join-russia.
10 'Decentralization', available at: https://decentralization.gov.ua/en/about.
11 Balázs Jarábik and Yulia Yesmukhanova, 'Ukraine's Slow Struggle for Decentralization', Carnegie Endowment for International Peace, 8 March 2017, available at: https://carnegieendowment.org/2017/03/08/ukraine-s-slow-struggle-for-decentralization-pub-68219.

7 History wars over the tragedies of the Soviet era

The famine (the Holodomor) that was artificially brought about by Stalinist agricultural policy from 1932 to 1933 is one of the greatest humanitarian catastrophes of the twentieth century. Stalin, who was from Georgia but who nonetheless treated his own nation just as brutally as all the other Soviet peoples, carried out the collectivisation of farming with an iron fist. In 1932 and 1933, there were, as a result, massive harvest failures in Ukraine and in southern Russia. The Commissars requisitioned all food supplies, including even the seeds for the following year. In their despair, the peasants slaughtered their cattle and could no longer till their fields. Entire villages died out; even cases of cannibalism emerged.

Much later, in 1968, the émigré historian Pavlo Shtepa coined the term 'Holodomor', a Ukrainian neologism which is composed of the elements *holod* ('hunger') and *moryty* ('to put to death').[1] In a book from 1978, the émigré author Vasyl Hryshko explicitly compared the 'Holodomor' to the Holocaust.[2] In 1988, shortly before the demise of the Soviet Union, the writer Oleksiy Musiyenko mentioned this term in a prominent position in his lecture at a writers' congress in Kyiv.[3] The term 'Holodomor' implies that the artificially induced famine represents a genocide, as the Soviet leadership wanted to exterminate the Ukrainian nation. The exact number of victims of the 'Holodomor' who died is still under debate. Recent research suggests some 3.9 million human losses, with a strong prevalence of mortality in rural areas.[4]

To this day, historians do not agree when it comes to the evaluation of this tragedy. In Ukraine, many researchers consider the Holodomor to have been a genocide of the Ukrainian people. Their main piece of evidence is a letter dated 11 August 1932 from Joseph Stalin to Lazar Kaganovich. Here the dictator writes:

> The most important issue right now is Ukraine. Things in Ukraine have hit rock bottom ... Unless we begin to straighten out the situation in Ukraine, we may lose Ukraine. Keep in mind that Piłsudski is not daydreaming ... Keep in mind, too, that the Ukrainian Communist Party (500,000 members, ha-ha) has quite a lot ... of rotten elements, conscious and unconscious Petliura adherents, and, finally, direct agents of

Piłsudski. As soon as things get worse, these elements will waste no time opening a front inside (and outside) the party, against the party. The worst aspect is that the Ukraine leadership does not see these dangers. Things cannot go on this way. We must ... set the goal of transforming Ukraine as quickly as possible into a real fortress of the USSR, into a genuinely exemplary republic. We should be unstinting in providing money.[5]

On the basis of such statements, it can indeed be said that the Soviet leadership was intensely concerned with Ukraine. However, it is probably difficult to deduce from this letter that Stalin intended to carry out a genocide of the Ukrainians. Clearly, Stalin wanted to press ahead with collectivisation, regardless of losses. At the beginning of 1933, Stalin's secret police received the order to put a stop to the flight of peasants who were searching for food. Some 220,000 people were arrested, of whom 190,000 were returned to their villages – where they starved to death. In the same year, the writer Mikhail Sholokhov engaged in a correspondence with Stalin and stood up for the starving population in the Don region. Stalin replied that the peasants themselves were responsible for this situation, since they had waged a 'secret war against Soviet power' and now had to face the consequences. In a perverse distortion of the facts, Stalin accused the supposedly counter-revolutionary peasants of 'deploying hunger as a weapon'.[6]

The Holodomor led to a reduction of the ethnic Ukrainian population of about 13 per cent. In contrast to the Holocaust, though, the famine that was artificially brought about by collectivisation in Ukraine was not organised so as to wipe out an entire ethnic group; and in the Holodomor, people were killed not directly but rather indirectly, by being deprived of sustenance. Ultimately, the motives for the Holodomor were not racist but political.

One should probably also take account of the fact that the Soviet power was, or at least claimed to be, directed against all nations in the domain over which it ruled. National identities were supposed to be replaced by a social identity. The most prominent conceptualisation of this process was Soviet patriotism, which was emphasised, in propaganda under Stalin, as a replacement for nationalist convictions. Soviet patriotism was set up on the basis of a 'socialist fatherland' that was supposed to supersede ethnic nationalism and create an idea of unity. In this sense Soviet patriotism was directed not only against Ukrainian nationalism but against all nationalisms in the entire Soviet Union; and also even extreme Russian nationalism was thereby affected. A case in point is the Russian nationalist Nikolay Vasilyevich Ustryalov (1890–1937). After the Bolshevik revolution, he had fled from Russia, but in the 1930s he mistook Stalin for a strong national leader, returned after this fateful decision to Moscow – and was shot during the Great Terror.

Under Stalin, however, a clear preference was shown towards the Russians among all the Soviet peoples. This privileged position could be seen most clearly in Stalin's famous toast after the victory over Nazi Germany:

> I should like to propose a toast to the health of our Soviet people, and in the first place, of the Russian people. I drink in the first place to the health of the Russian people because it is the most outstanding nation of all the nations forming the Soviet Union ...
>
> I propose a toast to the health of the Russian people not only because it is the leading people, but also because it possesses a clear mind, a staunch character, and patience.[7]

After the Orange Revolution of 2004, the government of Viktor Yushchenko put the Holodomor at the top of its agenda in terms of cultural policies. The diplomatic representatives of Ukraine carried out lobbying in many states, asking for a political recognition of the Holodomor. To date, the parliaments of Andorra, Argentina, Australia, Canada, Columbia, Ecuador, Slovakia and the United States have complied with this wish and recognised the Holodomor as a genocide of the Ukrainian people. Quite regardless of the generally questionable nature of such parliamentary decisions, which testify rather to efficient lobbying work than to informed judgements about a historical event, one must ask what the underlying reason is for the prominent positioning of this issue on the international stage. The answer probably lies in Ukrainian domestic politics. The Holodomor is suited, like no other historical event, to serve as justification for Ukraine taking on the collective identity of a victim. Precisely because the Holodomor took place on Soviet territory and affected not only Ukrainian but also Russian peasants, the catastrophic famine cannot be suspected of being a fabrication by Galician nationalists. In the post-heroic age at the end of the twentieth century and the beginning of the twenty-first, national identity is justified in many countries by means of discourses of victimisation. Israel and Armenia are of course prominent cases, but Poland and Serbia also strongly emphasise their own role as victims. Since the turn of the millennium, even people in Germany want to be emancipated from their dominant identity as perpetrators in the war: here important milestones are Guido Knopp's TV series *Die große Flucht* [*The Great Exodus*, 2001], which is concerned with the expulsion of Germans from the Eastern regions, Jörg Friedrich's book about the Allied bombing war, *The Fire* (2002),[8] and the anonymous diary *Eine Frau in Berlin* [*A Woman in Berlin*, 2003],[9] which, in a most distressing way, describes acts of rape by Soviet soldiers.

Under the presidency of Viktor Yanukovych, the issue of the Holodomor tended to be kept more in the background. Yanukovych wanted above all to avoid antagonising Russia, yet at the same time it was also clear to him that the Holodomor could have the effect of binding different regions together in social terms; and he therefore attempted to take over the issue himself. On 17 May 2010, along with Dmitry Medvedev, the Russian President at the time, Yanukovych laid a wreath at the Memorial to the Victims of the Holodomor near the Monastery of the Caves in Kyiv. One of the last official acts of Yushchenko before he relinquished the presidency had been to upgrade the status of this memorial to that of a national monument.

The focus on the Holodomor in the Ukrainian politics of memory has to a certain extent pushed the Holocaust into the background. In a speech in the Knesset in 2007, President Yushchenko went so far as to ask Israel to acknowledge the Holodomor as a genocide. The Holocaust on Ukrainian soil had already been a difficult topic during Soviet times. The official socialist remembrance did everything it could to avoid any particular victimisation of the Jews during the Second World War. The mass killing of 33,000 Kyivan Jews in Babi Yar, in September 1941, received an official monument only in 1976 – and the inscription, even then, spoke only about the murder of 'Soviet citizens' and 'prisoners of war'. This was the prescribed terminology for all massacres perpetrated by Nazi Germany or its ally Romania in Ukraine. Cases in point are the mass killings of Ukrainian Jews in Berdychiv, Kamianets-Podilskyi, Lviv, Odessa, Simferopol and Kharkiv. One of the first voices to draw attention to the painful topic of the Holocaust was the writer Vassily Grossman (1905–1964). His report 'Ukraine Without Jews' (1943) was turned down by the official newspaper of the Soviet Army, *Red Star*, and could be published only in a Yiddish translation in the much smaller periodical of the Jewish Antifascist Committee. In the decade after the demise of the Soviet Union, the Holocaust was hardly mentioned in Ukrainian public discourse. Textbooks treated the Holocaust as an event that took place abroad. Only after 2006 did the Holocaust appear as a topic for school exams in History. Today, the memory of the Holocaust in Ukraine is mostly left to non-governmental initiatives and civic organisations. The Holocaust museums in Kharkiv, Odessa and Dnipro are financed by private individuals.[10]

Even more controversial than the Holodomor, arguably, is the role of the Ukrainian Insurgent Army (UPA) during the Second World War. The UPA emerged, beginning in 1942, as the military wing of the 'Organisation of Ukrainian Nationalists' (OUN) that had been founded in Vienna in 1929. The goal of the OUN was the establishment of an independent Ukrainian state. Dmytro Dontsov (1883–1973), who maintained racist and fascist stances, may be considered the most important visionary of the OUN. However, Dontsov was never actually a member of the OUN – probably in order not to jeopardise his position as a journalist in the Second Polish Republic. He had already committed himself to the cause of an independent Ukraine at the end of the First World War, and had been active from 1919 to 1921 in the diplomatic representation of the 'Ukrainian People's Republic' in Bern. In the inter-war years, Dontsov published a Ukrainian newspaper with a markedly nationalistic orientation in Polish Lwów (Lemberg). He formulated the quintessence of his political views in his book *Nationalism* (1922).[11] Dontsov linked his own programme to a violent polemic against nineteenth-century Ukrainian national conceptions. The verdict he passed on Mykhailo Drahomanov was especially severe; eager to show deference, Drahomanov had seen Ukraine merely as one element in a federation with Russia. Dontsov also extended the accusation of 'Drahomanovism' to Nikolay Kostomarov and Panteleimon Kulish, both of whom had, according to Dontsov, contemplated the autonomy of Ukrainian culture but become stuck in their defeatist propositions about complementarity. Dontsov subsumed these various conceptions of Ukraine under the catchy slogan of 'Provençalism': this image of a harmless regional nature reserve in a cultural empire was aptly used by the centres of power, he wrote critically, to characterize the relationship between Provence and France and that between Ukraine and Russia.

A further parallel to the relationship between Russia and Ukraine lay in the hegemony of Prussia in the German Empire. Dontsov referred here to Friedrich Meinecke's book *Cosmopolitanism and the National State* (1908),[12] in which the dangers of imbalance in the case of a lopsided nation state dominated by one group are described. Dontsov argued for the sustainable emancipation of individual national cultures from the political dominance of a particular ethnic group that had declared itself to be a nation state. Drahomanov's key mistake, as Dontsov saw it, lay precisely in the recognition of this unjust *fait accompli*: Drahomanov thus became obliged to a foreign nation, namely, Russia, and just because of this stance, he failed to see the autochthonous truth of Ukraine.[13]

Dontsov himself repeatedly sank into a voluntaristic kind of pathos that he drew in the first instance from the writings of Friedrich Nietzsche. Dontsov quoted from the book *The Will to Power* (1906) that was compiled by Peter Gast and Elisabeth Förster-Nietzsche, in which Nietzsche is presented as an apologist for nationalistic dictatorship: 'We homeless ones from the very beginning – we have no choice at all, we must be conquerors and discoverers.'[14] This type of argument was a convenient one for Dontsov. A misfortune here could be positively reinterpreted as a virtue: if Ukraine had been oppressed from the very beginning, then the only way out that remained was warlike expansion. Dontsov's reading of Nietzsche, however, is completely superficial and can be compared to being similar to the interpretation of Nietzsche during the Nazi period whereby his work became propaganda for the Superman and for a rejection of the customary slave morality.[15] Paradoxically, Dontsov saw the most likely embodiment of Nietzsche's Superman in the figure of the Bolshevik Commissar. Dontsov was, of course, a sworn enemy of the Communists, yet at the same time he praised the Bolshevik 'will to power' as a formal model – a model, though, that was not connected to the correct political ideology until the time of Mussolini.

Dontsov's commentary on the seizure of power by Hitler in 1933 is also telling. Hitler, in this account, had put an end to the weak Weimar Republic and was carrying on the tradition of Frederick the Great;[16] Hitler was thus the first European leader who could compete directly with the Bolsheviks in decisiveness and vigour.[17] The opposition between Russia and Ukraine, though, took precedence for Dontsov over the opposition between Communism and Fascism. Russia not only was absolutely hostile towards Ukraine but also represented the Other and the foreign as such, and so, for Dontsov, the boundary between East and West ran not between the Russian Empire or the Soviet Union and Europe, but rather between Russia and Ukraine. As

Dontsov succinctly put it, Ukraine is thus not the westernmost point of the East but rather the easternmost point of the West.[18]

While Dontsov was creating the theoretical foundations for the actions of the OUN, Stepan Bandera (1909–1959) was engaging in acts of sabotage against the Polish occupying forces and against representatives of the Soviet Union. After the assassination of the Polish Minister of Internal Affairs, Bronisław Pieracki, in 1934, Bandera was arrested and initially condemned to death in Warsaw; but the death sentence was commuted to life imprisonment – and with the collapse of Poland in 1939, he was released. During the German Occupation, he collaborated with the Nazis, in order to gain their support for the formation of an independent state. He actively participated in the formation of both the Ukrainian Nazi battalions, 'Nachtigall' ('Nightingale') and 'Roland'; later in the war, the Ukrainian SS division 'Galicia' emerged from these units. Bandera and the Nazis parted ways, however, when a Ukrainian state was declared in Lviv on 30 June 1941. Bandera was arrested and spent the years from 1941 to 1944 in German prisons and in the Sachsenhausen concentration camp. Nevertheless, units of a Ukrainian Insurgent Army (the UPA) were formed in 1942, at first, fighting mainly against the Red Army but later also against the *Wehrmacht*. In 1942, members of the UPA participated in the killing of Jews in Volhynia, and a year later they carried out massacres of the Polish population there. The UPA continued its struggle against the Soviet forces after the official end of the war as well. In this context, Commander Roman Shukhevych (1907–1950) played an important role; he died on 5 March 1950 as a partisan, fighting against Soviet units near Lviv.

During the Soviet period, the OUN-UPA was a taboo issue, and the official historical narrative emphasised the heroic struggle of Soviet Ukraine against Nazi Germany. After the collapse of the Communist system, the situation changed dramatically. Opposing interpretations of history suddenly confronted each other: were the fighters of the UPA fascist traitors, or rather, the heroic pioneers of a Ukrainian state?

This debate became even fiercer because of President Yushchenko's policies concerning history. In 2007, he had declared UPA Commander Shukhevych to be a 'Hero of Ukraine', and in 2010, the same honour was accorded to Bandera. In 2009, in his decree 'On Additional Efforts Regarding the Recognition of the Ukrainian Liberation Movements of the Twentieth Century', Yushchenko gave the OUN and the UPA the blessing of formal state attention. However, the victor of the presidential elections in 2010, Viktor Yanukovych, promptly annulled Bandera's designation as a 'Hero of Ukraine' in January 2011. The Ukrainian Prime Minister Arseniy Yatsenyuk gave these debates a change of direction when, on 7 January 2015, he spoke in a TV interview for the German broadcaster ARD about an 'invasion of Germany and Ukraine by the Soviet Union'. Here he meant the advance of the Red Army after the defeat of the *Wehrmacht* at Stalingrad in January 1943 and the subsequent Sovietisation of the GDR as well as of Galicia and Bukovina.

President Putin immediately issued a statement: he would not allow attempts to be made to rewrite history. The Russian President firmly stuck to the Soviet interpretation whereby the Red Army had liberated Nazi-occupied Ukraine. In an act of retaliation, the Kyiv City Council decided in 2016 to rename one of its main arteries, the former 'Moscow Avenue', 'Bandera Avenue'.

The war of memory that rages around the figure of Stepan Bandera can also clearly be traced in the culture of monuments in Ukraine. Since 1990, above all in Galicia but more recently also in Volhynia, 46 monuments to Bandera have been erected. In Western Ukraine, over a hundred streets have been named after the nationalist leader. The monuments to Bandera often replaced the Soviet monuments to Lenin, to Felix Dzerzhinsky (founder of the Cheka), or to Red Army soldiers, that had become obsolete. Ironically enough, though, the new statues to Bandera repeat the aesthetic of the monuments to Lenin: both are honoured as the leaders of popular movements, and for such figures, because that is what the population is accustomed to see as monuments, they follow the traditional style.[19] On the other hand, hundreds of monuments to Lenin can still be found in Eastern Ukraine above all. Here, in the first instance, it is not even a question of honouring the cosmopolitan revolutionary, but rather of remembering his services to the Ukrainian cause. In a Soviet interpretation, Lenin was not responsible for the failure of the 'Ukrainian People's Republic' (UNR), but instead, on the contrary, is considered the founding father of the first stable Ukrainian state, the Ukrainian Soviet Republic.

Even the Ukrainian dissident Ivan Dziuba (born in 1931), in his banned polemic *Internationalism or Russification?* (1965), argued the case for Lenin, who had famously made an energetic appearance on the scene to oppose Great Russian chauvinism.[20] Because Lenin still represents an important figure for many Ukrainians, the Lenin monument in Kyiv, for instance, also remained untouched for a long time. It was not until 8 December 2013, in the early phase of the Euromaidan protests, that this Lenin monument was razed by Ukrainian activists. The same fate later befell the statues of Lenin in Mykolaiv and Kharkiv. In a survey, 69 per cent of the inhabitants of Kyiv who were asked spoke out against the overthrowing of the monument to Lenin in their city and were prepared to call it an act of vandalism. Paradoxically, a survey from March 2013 still yielded a majority of 62 per cent who did not want to preserve this prominent monument.[21] The high level of reluctance with regard to the toppling of the Lenin statue can be seen as the refusal of many citizens simply to throw away the Soviet period on the rubbish heap of history.

Since 2014, and especially since the adoption of the laws on de-communisation in 2015, almost 1,500 monuments to Lenin have been removed, mostly in the eastern and southern parts of Ukraine. In Western Ukraine, monuments to Lenin had already been destroyed in the early 1990s.

The Russian aggression has led to a situation whereby Ukraine increasingly wants to distance itself from Russia. On 15 May 2015, President Poroshenko signed a package of four so-called 'de-communisation laws' that had been supported in Parliament by most of the leading parties.[22] The first law, concerning 'the legal status and honouring the memory of the Ukrainian freedom fighters of the twentieth century', consists of a conclusive list of organisations which distinguished themselves in the cause of Ukrainian independence. The safeguarding of their memory is now the task of the state; and a 'disparaging attitude' to these freedom fighters was made a criminal offence. Equally forbidden is any public questioning of the legitimacy of the Ukrainian struggle for independence. The second law regulates the 'immortalisation of the victory over Nazism in the Second World War'. Here Ukraine is represented as a double victim, of both National Socialist and Soviet aggression. The 'honouring remembrance' of the veterans of the war, of the Ukrainian liberation fighters and of the war's victims is now a 'sacred duty' of the state and of Ukrainian citizens. Whoever fails to abide by these principles will be punished. The third law opens up access to the archives of the 'repressive organs of the totalitarian Communist regime from 1917 to 1991'. Every citizen now has an unrestricted right to consult the files of the secret services. The fourth law, finally, condemns the 'totalitarian Communist and National Socialist regimes' and forbids 'the propagation of their imagery'. The depiction not only of the swastika but also of the Soviet emblem with its hammer and sickle is thereby made a criminal offence. Moreover, all place and street names that recall Communist ideology must be changed.

All four of these laws are highly problematic and raise more questions than they purport to solve. The laws are based on an antiquated understanding of history that assumes the existence of an 'objective' historical truth. Furthermore, in their conception of totalitarianism, they equate Soviet Communism with National Socialism and thus revert to the position of historiography as it was in the 1950s. The discussion of the fundamental principle whether the state should get involved with historical research at all is lacking in Ukraine. At least two reasons can be given against such an involvement: first, the image of history that Members of Parliament have, as a rule, is not founded on their competence in the subject but rather on their respective party ideology; and, second, historiography is a dynamic discipline, the outcomes of which are constantly being adjusted according to the historical sources that are currently available. To enshrine one particular interpretation of history, and to criminalise alternative narratives, is a contradiction of academic freedom, in which not a so-called 'sacred duty' but rather a principled scepticism should represent the guiding precept of research.

The first law in the 2015 package presumes to name, by decree, all the pioneers of Ukrainian independence. Especially striking here is the fact that both the 'Organisation of Ukrainian Nationalists' (OUN) and the 'Ukrainian Insurgent Army' (UPA) figure on the list of freedom fighters to be honoured. The UPA had of course distinguished itself in the struggle for independence in particular, and its partisan attacks on the Soviet regime carried on into the 1950s. At the same time, the question as to whether all means to achieve political independence were really permissible must also be raised; for the UPA had, to some extent, collaborated with the Nazis in the Second World War, had made itself partly responsible for the Holocaust, and had carried out a massacre of the Polish civilian population in Volhynia.

The second law undertakes a difficult balancing act between a cult of remembrance of the victory over Nazi Germany, with Soviet characteristics, and a new discourse of victimhood which takes Ukraine to be a territory that was occupied by the Soviets. This law hereby splits up the Soviet past into a good part and a bad part: the Soviet victory in the Second World War may be celebrated once more, but at the same time Ukraine also becomes a victim of Soviet aggression. Moreover, the Ukrainian Government is adamant in separating its celebration of victory in the Second World War from the corresponding manifestations in Russia. For the Kremlin, the military parades on 9 May continue the Soviet tradition and mark the most important historical date in the official culture of remembrance. In Ukraine, meanwhile, the Soviet term 'Great Patriotic War' was officially changed to 'World War II' in 2015, and at the same time a new 'Day of Remembrance and Reconciliation', to be celebrated on 8 May, was introduced. The Victory Day on 9 May continues to be an event in Ukrainian public culture. However, the Ukrainian symbols clearly differ from the Russian ones: instead of the Ribbon of St George, which consists of black and orange stripes and has become a symbol not only of Soviet victory in the war but also of public support of the Kremlin's policies, the Ukrainians sport button badges with a poppy seed symbol.

The third law cuts off any political debate in society about lustration, i.e., the purging of government officials, in Ukraine. Of course it seems desirable that the files of the secret services that were active in Ukraine should be made accessible. At the same time, though, the social damage that could be caused by an unregulated opening of the archives, just twenty-four years after the end of Communist rule, is potentially enormous. Defamations and character assassinations cannot be excluded if the names of informants or spies, torn out of context, are made public. Ultimately, it is also problematic that the conservative 'Ukrainian Institute of National Remembrance' has declared itself to be the unique keeper of the Holy Grail, the archival collections themselves. Here the danger exists that academic investigation of political repression in Ukraine will merely reconfirm the sense of victimisation that characterises official discourse.

The fourth law has the most far-reaching consequences. The website of the 'Institute of National Remembrance' lists over 900 villages and places that have to be renamed.[23] The number of names of town districts, metro stations and streets that are no longer permissible runs into the thousands. Even two cities can no longer keep their names, Dnipropetrovsk (with 990,000 inhabitants) and Kirovohrad (with 240,000 inhabitants). The absurdity of this law is shown to its full extent in the plan to rename the city of Dnipropetrovsk as 'Dnepropetrovsk'. The city was founded by Tsarina Catherine the Great as Ekaterinoslav; since 1926, it has been called Dnipropetrovsk, in memory of the Party functionary Grigory Petrovsky. The city council advocated the homonymous city name of Dnipropetrovsk and wanted simply to substitute the name of one city patron for another: instead of a relatively little-known Bolshevik, one is supposed to refer now to the Apostle Peter. This sleight of hand draws some justification from the history of architecture: Catherine's favourite, Prince Grigory Potemkin, had the Transfiguration Cathedral in Ekaterinoslav built after the model of St Peter's Basilica in the Vatican. On 19 May 2016, though, the Ukrainian Parliament decided to adopt the short form 'Dnipro' as the new city name.

In the current situation it is very dangerous to declare one nationalistic version of history to be the only truth. Ukraine possesses a complex history that is interpreted very differently in its individual regions. Many members of the older generation in the East of the country still describe themselves as Soviet citizens and cherish the Communist legacy.

There is, however, one historical figure who is honoured to the same extent in all regions of Ukraine, namely, the national poet, Taras Shevchenko (1814–1861). In other European cultures, such national poets have been dead for a long time and live on, at best, in compulsory readings in school. The case of Shevchenko is different, and in the last twenty years countless monuments have been erected to the national poet in Ukraine. His volume of poems, *Kobzar*, [24] has, in numerous new editions, a secure place in the display windows of Ukrainian bookshops.

Shevchenko's outstanding position can be explained by the fact that his work and his biography have diverse aspects that can be made current according to need. He was originally a serf and could thus be appropriated as a proletarian by Soviet culture. He wrote his prose in Russian and his poetry in Ukrainian, and is thus thought to be the embodiment of Ukrainian bilingualism. He wrote fierce poems against the oppression of the Ukrainian people by the Russian Tsars, and was thus also compatible with the programme of the Ukrainian nationalists. He spent a long time in St Petersburg and is thus also a factor in Russian culture.[25] Portraits of Shevchenko were widely displayed during the Euromaidan protests, and his poems were recited and set to music. Shevchenko serves as a symbol of 'Ukrainianness' without the need to define what Ukrainianness actually means.

Notes

1 Yaroslav Hrytsak, 'Khto i koly vpershe vzhiv slovo *Holodomor*?', 24 November 2017, available at: http://uamoderna.com/blogy/yaroslav-griczak/etymology-holodomor.
2 Vasyl Hryshko, *The Ukrainian Holocaust of 1933* (Toronto, 1983); the Ukrainian original appeared in 1978.
3 Anne Applebaum, *Red Famine: Stalin's War on Ukraine* (New York, 2017). Anne Applebaum notes that the word 'Haladamor' appears in Czech publications of the Ukrainian diaspora in the 1930s.
4 Oleh Wolowyna, Serhii Plokhy, Nataliia Levchuk, Omelian Rudnytskyi, Alla Kovbasiuk and Pavlo Shevchuk, 'Regional Variations of 1932–34 Famine Losses

in Ukraine', *Canadian Studies in Population*, XLIII (2016), pp. 175–202, pp. 175 and 185.
5 Joseph Stalin and Lazar Kaganovich, *The Stalin-Kaganovich Correspondence, 1931–1936*, trans. Steven Shabad, ed. R. W. Davies et al. (New Haven, CT, 2003), pp. 179–181.
6 Andrea Graziosi, 'The Soviet 1931–1933 Famines and the Ukrainian Holodomor: Is a New Interpretation Possible and What Would Its Consequences Be?', in *Hunger by Design*, ed. Halyna Hryn (Cambridge, 2008), pp. 1–13; p. 9.
7 Christopher Read, *Stalin: From the Caucasus to the Kremlin* (New York, 2017), p. 294.
8 Jörg Friedrich, *The Fire: The Bombing of Germany, 1940–1945*, trans. Allison Brown (New York, 2008).
9 Anonymous, *Eine Frau in Berlin: Tagebuchaufzeichnungen vom 20. April bis 22. Juni 1945* (Berlin, 2015).
10 Georgiy Kas'ianov, *Past Continuous: Istorychna polityka 1980-kh-2000-kh, Ukraina ta susidy* (Kyiv, 2018), pp. 283–288.
11 Dmytro Dontsov, *Nacionalizm* (L'viv, 1922), p. 171.
12 Friedrich Meinecke, *Cosmopolitanism and the National State*, trans. Robert B. Kimber (Princeton, NJ, 1970).
13 Dmytro Dontsov, *De shukati nashych tradytsii?* (L'viv, 1938), p. 44.
14 *Der Wille zur Macht, 1884–88: Versuch einer Umwerthung aller Werthe*, ed. Elisabeth Förster-Nietzsche and Peter Gast (Leipzig, 1906). See Mazzino Montinari, 'Nietzsche's Unpublished Writings from 1885 to 1888; or, Textual Criticism and the Will to Power', in Mazzino Montinari, *Reading Nietzsche*, trans. Greg Whitlock (Urbana, IL, 2003).
15 See Steven E. Aschheim, *The Nietzsche Legacy in Germany, 1890–1990* (Berkeley, CA, 1992).
16 Dmytro Dontsov, 'Zhoda w simejstvi', *Vistnyk*, VII–VIII (1936), pp. 598–602.
17 Dmytro Dontsov, 'Sumerk marksysmu (Tarde, Gitler, Stalins'ka oposycija, i my)', *Vistnyk*, I–II (1933), pp. 299–308; p. 304.
18 Dmytro Dontsov, *Pidstavy nashoi polityki* (Vienna, 1921), p. 74.
19 Andre Liebich and Oksana Myshlovska, 'Bandera: Memorialization and Commemoration', *Nationalities Papers: The Journal of Nationalism and Ethnicity*, XLII/5 (2014), pp. 750–770, available at: http://dx.doi.org/10.1080/00905992.2014.916666.
20 Ivan M. Dzjuba, *Internacionalizm ili rusifikacija?* (Kyiv, 1998), p. 241.
21 Oleksandra Gaidai, *Kam'jannyi hist': Lenin u tsentral'nyi Ukraini* (Kyiv, 2018), pp. 177f.
22 Andrii Portnov, 'How to Bid Goodbye to Lenin in Ukraine', *Open Democracy*, 26 May 2015, available at: www.opendemocracy.net/andriy-portnov/on-'decommunisation'-'identity'-and-legislating-history-in-ukraine.
23 Ukrains'kii instytut natsional'noi pam'iati, 'Rekomendatsii do pereimenuvannia', available at: www.memory.gov.ua/rename.
24 Taras Shevchenko, *Kobzar*, trans. Vera Rich (Kyiv, 2013).
25 Jenny Alwart, *Mit Taras Ševčenko Staat machen: Erinnerungskultur und Geschichtspolitik in der Ukraine vor und nach 1991* (Cologne, 2012).

8   The Ukraine crisis
Civil war or Russian hybrid war?

The war in Donbas that broke out shortly after the annexation of Crimea has hitherto claimed the lives of thousands of victims on both sides. It is difficult to comprehend this war in all its aspects. Certainly the official Russian interpretation, whereby Moscow denies being a warring party at all, is false. The inversion of this argument, though, is not simply admissible either; it cannot readily be claimed that there is no civil war taking place in Ukraine. Ukrainian citizens have killed other Ukrainian citizens. In November 2016, the Office of the Prosecutor of the International Criminal Court in The Hague assessed the military situation as an 'international armed' conflict between Russia and Ukraine which parallels a 'non-international armed conflict' in eastern Ukraine.[1]

Having said that, Russia is still the decisive factor in the war in Ukraine: Moscow aims to take control of Donbas away from the Government in Kyiv for a long time, and thus to drive a thorn into the flesh of Ukraine. This process follows the pattern of Russian aggression in Transnistria, South Ossetia and Abkhazia. These territories are still claimed by Moldova and Georgia, but any further integration of these states with the West is not possible without resolving their territorial conflicts.

The annexation of Crimea and the aggression in Donbas that followed shortly after were very probably not spontaneous decisions on the part of the Kremlin. The 'political engineer' Gleb Pavlovsky (born in 1951) is an insider in the world of power politics, and from 2000 to 2008 he worked on numerous media projects in order to generate public approval for Putin's Government. In 2011, however, he was deeply disappointed by the decision that only Putin would run for President, and he turned away from the Kremlin. Since then, he has become one of the fiercest critics of the government, always talking contemptuously about his own country as 'the system RF' (where RF stands for the 'Russian Federation'). At the end of March 2014, Pavlovsky said in an interview with the *Moscow Times*:

> The annexation of Crimea was a well worked-out plan; it is impossible to send special units of the military Secret Service into foreign territory without a plan. The fact that the operation was carried out brilliantly

proves that this plan had been sketched out a long time ago and stored for years by the General Staff.[2]

The plans for the annexation of Crimea may have come about in 2008, after the Russian *Blitzkrieg* against Georgia, when Yushchenko was advocating that Ukraine should join NATO. Individual Western politicians, such as the French Foreign Minister Bernard Kouchner and the Finnish EU Commissioner Olli Rehn, had already warned at that time that Putin's craving for territorial expansion could be directed next towards Crimea.

The annexation of Crimea was a textbook example of 'hybrid warfare'. This concept, according to NATO analysts, means an 'effective, often surprising mix of military and non-military, conventional and irregular components, and can include all kind of instruments such as cyber and information operations'.[3] After the Russian aggression against Ukraine, military experts drew attention to a lecture that General Valery Gerasimov (born in 1955), Chief of the General Staff of the Russian armed forces, had given in early 2013 at a conference at the Military Academy of the General Staff.[4] Gerasimov explained that the methods of warfare in the twenty-first century had been fundamentally transformed. Traditional forms such as the 'frontal collision of large groups', the 'rigorous conquest of precisely delimited territories' or the 'annihilation of the opponent' no longer applied. It was now much more a question of the 'deployment of political, diplomatic, economic and other non-military measures in combination with the application of military power'. Gerasimov here explicitly mentioned large-scale military manoeuvres without enemy contact, the specific deployment of special forces, asymmetrical and indirect attacks, as well as the extension of information warfare.

All these elements were deployed in the undeclared war that Russia waged on Ukraine. Pro-Russian provocations in Crimea, directed above all against the Tatar population, had already increased in 2012. At the end of February 2014, soldiers without insignia suddenly appeared in Crimea and staged themselves as silent protectors and saviours. They permitted young women to take selfies with them; and these pictures were disseminated on TV and via social media. By means of this management of public sympathy, the Russian interpretation of the conflict was supported, according to which it was necessary to protect the supposedly persecuted and oppressed Russians in Crimea from Ukrainian abuses.[5]

A further element of Russian warfare consisted in maintaining the semblance of legality. On 1 March 2014, Putin allowed himself to be given the authorisation by the Federation Council to deploy the army outside Russia. At this session of the Federation Council, which was widely broadcast, there was not a single speaker who expressed concern about Putin's plan. The President's application was unanimously approved, and the session was brought to an end by the national anthem being played. It was not that the Russian President had all of a sudden taken seriously the constitutional separation of powers; in the war against Georgia, in 2008, the Federation Council was not consulted until two weeks after the Russian invasion. In the case of Ukraine, the dramatic decision by the Federation Council – staged prominently in the media – allowed Putin to build up a threatening backdrop that did not fail to achieve its effect both inside and outside Russia.

On 24 May 2014, in a meeting with foreign journalists, Putin insisted that he considered Yanukovych to be, as he had been, the legitimate President of Ukraine:

> You know, we can all read. Let's open the constitution and read it. We are grown-up people, we can read. Take the Ukrainian constitution and read it. It says that there are four legitimate reasons when an incumbent president has to go. They are: death, a serious health condition, impeachment – and there was no constitution-based impeachment – and resignation, when the president hands in his resignation to the parliament. So we either stick to the constitution or dismiss it.[6]

In this statement, it is Putin's sustained insistence on Russian respect for the Constitution that is most important. In his criticism of the dismissal of the Ukrainian President, in terms of formal legality, the claim is also reflected that Putin himself is acting strictly in accordance with the letter of the law.

Russian propaganda was mobilised immediately after the annexation of Crimea. The range of devices deployed in the media extended from clumsy falsification via fictionalised emotional manipulation up to the melodramatic composition of entire sequences. At the beginning of March 2014, for instance, a contribution to the TV evening news on Channel One Russia itself made headlines. It was asserted here that 140,000 refugees from Ukraine had already arrived in Russia. Images of a long column at a border crossing flickered across the screen. Rather stupidly, the forgers had forgotten to remove the place name sign from the picture – and so it was an easy matter to expose the vehicles that were shown as a perfectly normal queue waiting to exit the country at the border with Poland. On 16 May 2014, the TV channel Russia One broadcast a piece in which a pro-Russian activist from Sloviansk was shown who had supposedly been shot by the National Guard of Ukraine. The footage used for this news announcement, though, derived from an earlier report on the same channel, in 2012; and ironically enough, at that time it was a unit of the Russian special forces that had liquidated a terrorist from the Northern Caucasus.

In order to put a human face to the oppression of Russians in Ukraine, resort was made to the services of an actress who was identified by investigative journalists as a certain Maria Tsipko. She appeared on Russian television in various roles: first of all, she collected donations for the pro-Russian camp in Odessa, then she made an appearance as a courageous citizen from Kharkiv bringing bread rolls and home-made jam to the fighters of the Berkut (the 'Eagle', a special police force) in Kyiv, later she became involved as a vote counter for the popular referendum in Luhansk, and finally, as a despairing refugee in Moscow, she denounced conditions in Ukraine.

Particular news items were not only manipulated by Russia but also fed into the flux of events virtually as show elements. Looking at it more closely, the dramaturgy of the Ukraine crisis resembles that of a modern TV series, produced according to all the rules of cinematic art. The first series began as a political drama, showing the President acting responsibly before the Federation Council. The genre subsequently changed to science fiction: out of nowhere, 'little green men' emerged in Crimea. As with intruders from Mars, at first no-one knew if they were dangerous or if one could trust them. This carefully built-up moment of suspense was then dispelled in quick-motion mode: within the space of a few days, in a series of thunderbolts, there came the referendum, the declaration of independence and the annexation by Russia. This episode had its triumphal finale in Putin's great speech before the Duma on 18 March 2014, in which he celebrated Holy Russia. At once a revolutionary play now came into the foreground. The Kremlin chose as a stage the 'typical small town' of Sloviansk. Here a new Danton appeared as protagonist, namely, the 'People's Mayor' Vyacheslav Ponomarev. As sub-plot, a hostage drama was built in that soon turned out, however, to be a provincial farce. Subsequently, as a war drama, there followed an episode called 'Civil War': professionally equipped fighters in spotted camouflage and black face masks were shooting at an anonymous enemy, of whom the armoured vehicles were the most that was visible. As the personification of this heroic resistance, there appeared the intelligence officer Igor Girkin (born in 1970), shrouded in secrecy, who became famous under his romantic *nom de guerre* Strelkov ('Shooter'); thanks to his military decisiveness, his conspicuously displayed religiosity and his patriotic war poetry, Strelkov quickly advanced to become a cult figure for the most far-right groups in Russia. Pro-Russian civilians could be seen, as extras, bravely standing up to the Ukrainian military entourage.

In parallel to this TV series, the Russian aggression was also reinforced by historical arguments. The concept of *Novorossiya* ('New Russia'), already prominently positioned by President Putin in his *Direct Line with Vladimir Putin* TV programme on 17 April 2014, played an important role in this reinforcement. Putin referred to the fact that it was Russia's task to protect the 'rights and interests of the Russian and Russian-speaking citizens of South-Eastern Ukraine'. Putin continued:

> I would like to remind you that what was called Novorossiya [New Russia] back in the Tsarist days – Kharkov, Lugansk, Donetsk, Kherson, Nikolayev and Odessa – were not part of Ukraine back then. These territories were given to Ukraine in the 1920s by the Soviet government. Why? Who knows? They were won by Potyomkin and Catherine the Great in a series of well-known wars. The centre of that territory was Novorossiysk, so the region is called Novorossiya. Russia lost these territories for various reasons, but the people remained.[7]

The argumentation of the Russian President thus amounted to proposing that to some extent the ground had been pulled out from under the feet of the

'Russian and Russian-speaking' population of New Russia, but that their ethnic origin remained Russian nonetheless. Putin thereby further exacerbated the ethnic dimensions of the conflict: in this reading of it, 'Russians' in 'New Russia' were fighting for their legitimate historical heritage against the 'Ukrainian usurpers'.[8]

The performance of intimidating manoeuvres also played an important role in the Russian style of warfare. In the latter half of March 2014, the Kremlin concentrated an army with the strength of about 80,000 men, with hundreds of tanks, at the border with Ukraine. The West subsequently behaved exactly as the Kremlin had intended. On 23 March 2014, the US General Philip M. Breedlove, the Supreme Allied Commander in Europe, stepped up before the assembled media and explained that the Russian troops at the border 'had reached a considerable size' and were 'very, very much ready for action'.[9] Breedlove warned of a Russian march through Ukraine all the way to Transnistria. Given this statement, the war was in fact already won for Russia. The mere images of marching troops already had the same effect as an actual invasion; and as long as the West was afraid of the Russian tanks, Putin had no need to set them in motion.

A further part of Moscow's strategy consisted in maintaining the pretence of not being involved in this war at all. In diplomatic jargon, this approach is called 'plausible deniability'. Care is taken, following this strategy, so as to be able to present oneself with plausible reasons in public as if one were uninformed about, or uninvolved in, a particular chain of events. At first, this strategy seemed to be working. In Moscow, there was a consistent discourse about 'people's militias' and 'self-defence units' that were supposed to be fighting against the Ukrainian army. In the course of conflicts that took place in the war, however, it became increasingly clear that members of the Russian armed forces were fighting on Ukrainian soil. On at least two occasions, President Putin himself seemed to admit to a Russian military presence in Ukraine. During a press meeting on 17 December 2015, Putin slyly maintained: 'We never said there were not people there who carried out certain tasks including in the military sphere.' The initial part of this sentence, of course, was a blatant lie. On 4 June 2014, Putin had asserted the opposite in an interview with French journalists: 'There are no armed forces, no Russian instructors in southeastern Ukraine. And there never were any.'[10] The second instance was a statement at the investment forum *Russia Calling* on 12 October 2016. Putin said probably in a slip of the tongue: 'We were obliged to protect the population in the Donbas.' In the next sentence, he jumped to Crimea as a topic, probably because he had just remembered that the official stance was still that Russia had not interfered in Eastern Ukraine.

The shooting down of the Malaysian passenger aircraft (flight MH17), on 17 July 2014, marked a turning point. Special forces with heavy anti-aircraft batteries from the regular inventory of the Russian army were probably responsible for this calamity. Most probably, the downing of the civilian plane was not a deliberate attack but rather an error: the separatists had thus taken the passenger aircraft to be a Ukrainian military jet.

This air disaster abruptly gave the conflict a new dimension. The EU agreed, remarkably quickly, on economic sanctions; previously, sanctions had only been imposed that restricted personal travel and movements of capital for individuals in Putin's inner circle of leadership.

Events in the embattled small town Ilovaisk marked an important turning point in military terms. The Ukrainian army had carried out a successful advance against the separatists in August 2014, but it was then beaten back by regular Russian troops with heavy weapons and tanks. Since Ilovaisk, it is clear that every Ukrainian military action will be countered on the Russian side by the deployment of the most up-to-date military equipment. In February 2015, this situation was repeated in the strategically important town Debaltseve, which lies exactly between Donetsk and Luhansk. It is thus highly unlikely that the territories held by the separatists in Donbas will be recaptured.

The so-called Minsk Protocol of 5 September 2014, furthermore, was signed under the most inauspicious circumstances. The main success of this mission, in which the Organisation for Security and Co-operation in Europe (OSCE) aimed to mediate, was the inclusion of the Russian side. In the text of this agreement it is therefore not so much the content that is important but rather the list of signatories: for the OSCE, the Swiss special ambassador Heidi Tagliavini signed; for Ukraine, the former President, Leonid Kuchma; for Russia, the ambassador to Kyiv, Mikhail Zurabov; and the signatures of the two separatist leaders Alexander Zakharchenko and Igor Plotnitsky followed, without official titles. Both Moscow and Kyiv had to distance themselves from their own positions here. For the Kremlin, the signature of the Ambassador meant an admission of having some involvement in the conflict; the Ukrainian Government refused for a long time to take a place at the negotiating table with the rebel leaders at all.

The events of winter 2014–2015 showed that the Minsk Protocol could not guarantee a cessation of hostilities. The problem of the agreement lies in the fact that the interests of the separatists and the interests of the central government in Kyiv could not be aligned by any means. As a compromise, the Minsk Protocol made provisions for the creation of a 'special status in individual districts of the Donetsk and Luhansk regions', but this was both too little for the separatists and too much for Kyiv.

Since the situation in Eastern Ukraine was not improving, Angela Merkel, François Hollande, Vladimir Putin and Petro Poroshenko met on 11 February 2015 in Minsk, in order to discuss a comprehensive peace agreement. The concluding text, though, was signed not by the heads of state but merely by the negotiating partners from the first Minsk Protocol. The second Minsk agreement ('Minsk II'), in essence, makes provisions for constitutional reform in Ukraine in the first instance; only after that would Ukraine again be able to exert complete control over the border between Russia and Ukraine.

One structural problem of the Minsk agreements lies in the fact that any compromise that is within reach at all already represents a war aim on the part of Moscow. For Russia, it is a matter of destabilising the whole of Ukraine and of derailing Ukrainian statehood in Donbas. The rapprochement of Ukraine with the EU or with NATO should thereby be made so unattractive to Western organisations that, in the end, Ukraine will return to Moscow's economic and political sphere of influence.

There are, however, also far-reaching implications of the Ukrainian conflict for Russia itself. In 2018, Crimea's adherence to Russia took on material form with the construction of a 19-kilometre-long bridge from the Russian mainland to the peninsula. This new connection not only allows for better and cheaper logistics, but also reinforces Russian control over the Sea of Azov. Traffic at the Ukrainian ports of Berdyansk and Mariupol has decreased considerably due to bureaucratic harassment by Russian Border Patrol boats. On 25 November 2018, this tense situation even acquired a military dimension. In the Russian reading of events, three Ukrainian Navy vessels had violated 'Russian territorial waters' in the Kerch Strait. From a Ukrainian point of view, there is no Russian jurisdiction near the Crimea. The Ukrainian vessels should have had the right to pass through the Kerch Strait as convened in a treaty between Russia and Ukraine of 2003. In this document, the Sea of Azov was declared an internal water for both states, with free passage for all ships. However, it was in the interests of neither side to escalate this incident to a fully-fledged war: Russia did not want to abandon its rhetorical strategy of not being a war party, while Ukraine knew very well that any military confrontation with its powerful neighbour would inevitably lead to a miserable failure.

Russia's military power is a kind of trump card that loses its effect the very moment when it is played. The Kremlin likes to pose as a strong government that defends the rights of its citizens, at home and also abroad. However, the double strategy of annexing Crimea and instigating a violent conflict in Donbas leads to a discursive dilemma. Why does Russia not intervene in Donbas in just the way it has intervened in Crimea? From a strategic perspective, the answer is clear: the status quo is exactly what serves the Kremlin's interests best. For this reason, the Kremlin spares no effort to keep this critical question from even being asked.

Drawing up an interim balance for Russia's aggression against Ukraine leads to a divided result. On the one hand, parts of Putin's plan have worked out: the statehood of Ukraine as such has been substantially unsettled. The return of Crimea to Ukraine appears to be highly unlikely in the foreseeable future. At least initially, Putin emerged from 2014 with a strengthened position in terms of domestic politics; and his approval ratings, following the annexation of Crimea, moved up to the fabulous level of 85 per cent. In the meantime, the initial enthusiasm in the Russian public sphere has worn into a general consensus that Crimea is and should remain Russian. Approval rates for President Putin have dropped to a mere 66 per cent, after the announcement of the widely unpopular pension age reform in 2018.

On the other hand, ranks have closed in Ukraine following the Russian aggression. It was not only Russia but also Ukraine that was caught up in a wave of patriotism in 2014. A survey that was carried out in all the regions of Ukraine (apart from Crimea), in August 2014, produced a rate of 86 per cent agreement in response to the question: 'Do you describe yourself as a patriot of your country?'[11] In September 2010, only 76 per cent of those asked had answered this question in the affirmative. The detailed figures from Donbas are especially interesting: here, against the background of the belligerent events that had taken place, it was above all the group of those undecided and at a loss that had grown strongly. So, in August 2014, admittedly 69 per cent of those asked in Donbas still described themselves as Ukrainian patriots, but every fifth person would not respond either affirmatively or negatively to the question. This trend was seen even more clearly in the case of the question: 'Would you support Ukraine's declaration of independence again today?' In Western Ukraine, predictably, 99 per cent of respondents answered this question in the affirmative in August 2014. In Donbas, by contrast, three groups of roughly the same size arose: 34 per cent would be for, another 34 per cent would be against, and at the same time a rather large group, 31 per cent of those asked, preferred not to commit themselves one way or the other. In August 2012, by way of comparison, only just 32 per cent in Donbas had supported the independence of Ukraine; 57 per cent were against the idea, and a mere 11 per cent preferred not to answer the question.

The investigation showed, moreover, that the independence of Ukraine was supported by relatively young, well-educated and affluent citizens who declared Ukrainian to be their mother tongue. On the other hand, though, only 30 per cent of Russian-speaking Ukrainians rejected the independence of the country; 45 per cent supported the idea, and 25 per cent were undecided. Equally striking is the relatively high approval of Ukrainian independence on the part of those people who do not describe themselves as Ukrainian patriots (34 per cent).

Ukraine has consequently moved together as a nation. An index of social distance from 2017 shows that Ukrainians feel socially close to each other, regardless of their language. Ukrainians express more social distance to Russians than to Belarussians, but Russians still rank above Poles, Jews or Crimean Tatars in this sense: 16 per cent of the Ukrainians surveyed would accept Russians as family members, 14 per cent would accept them as friends, 20 per cent would accept them as neighbours, while 13 per cent would not let them enter Ukraine at all.[12] Regional differences persist, as was the case before. The results of the survey show that meanwhile, in Donbas, no majority of the population is advocating an annexation by Russia. In the regions most affected by the crisis, in the easternmost part of Ukraine, a general sense of being at a loss has spread. Many people trust neither Moscow nor Kyiv, and all promises of salvation have lost their credibility in Donbas. In the regions occupied by the separatists, it is in any case only those people who could not be saved by relatives or friends in central Ukraine or in Russia who have remained behind. Valuable infrastructure, including that set up in the context of the UEFA European Championship in 2012, lies in ruins. The brand-new airport terminal in Donetsk, similarly, has been completely destroyed. Schools and university buildings have been damaged, and teaching activities are possible only under precarious conditions.

Notes

1 'Report on Preliminary Examination Activities 2016', 14 November 2016, p. 37, available at: www.icc-cpi.int/iccdocs/otp/161114-otp-rep-PE_ENG.pdf.
2 Yekaterina Kravtsova, 'Observers Say Russia Had Crimea Plan for Years', *The Moscow Times*, 27 March 2014, available at: www.themoscowtimes.com/news/article/observers-say-russia-had-crimea-plan-for-years/496936.html.
3 Heidi Reisinger and Alexander Golts, *Russia's Hybrid Warfare: Waging War Below the Radar of Traditional Collective Defence*, NATO Research Paper 105 (Rome, 2014), available at: www.ndc.nato.int/news/news.php?icode=732.
4 Valerii Gerasimov, 'Tsennost' nauki v predvidenii', *Voenno-promyshlennyi kur'er*, 26 February 2013, available at: www.vpk-news.ru/articles/14632.
5 Douglas Becker, 'The Rationality and Emotion of Russian Historical Memory: The Case of Crimea', in *Crisis and Change in Post-Cold War Global Politics: Ukraine in a Comparative Perspective*, ed. Erica Resende *et al.* (Cham, 2018), pp. 43–69.
6 Vladimir Putin, speech at meeting with Heads of Leading International News Agencies, 24 May 2014, available at: http://en.kremlin.ru/events/president/news/21090.
7 Direct Line with Vladimir Putin, 17 April 2014, available at: http://en.kremlin.ru/events/president/news/20796. It should be noted here that Kharkiv was never part of the historical region of 'Novorossiya'.
8 Gerard Toal, *Near Abroad: Putin, the West, and the Contest over Ukraine and the Caucasus* (New York, 2017), pp. 237–273.
9 'NATO Commander Warns of Russian Threat to Separatist Moldova Region', *Reuters*, 23 March 2014, available at: www.reuters.com/article/2014/03/23/ukraine-crisis-idUSL5N0MK0D020140323.
10 Vladimir Putin, interview with Radio Europe 1 and TF1 TV Channel, 1 June 2014, available at: http://en.kremlin.ru/events/president/news/45832.
11 'Dynamika patriotychnykh nastroiv, Serpen'' 2014 (Kyiv, 2014), available at: http://ratinggroup.ua/files/ratinggroup/reg_files/rg_patriotyzm_082014.pdf.
12 Survey, 'Post-Maidan Ukraine (2015 and 2017)', available at: www.uaregio.org/en/surveys/data-visualisations/survey-infographics/post-maidan-ukraine-2015/.

9 The Ukrainian economy

Ukraine once used to be considered the breadbasket of Russia. Vast expanses of land have valuable black earth. Today, agriculture is still an important branch of the Ukrainian economy, above all on the fertile plains of western and central Ukraine. Ukraine is Europe's biggest producer of grains, and it is even a world leader in the production of beer barley and of cooking oil. In the East, coal mining and the steel industry dominate; in this region, though, dilapidated facilities (mostly deriving from the Soviet era) make it difficult to achieve profitable and ecologically sustainable production. A particular feature of the Ukrainian economy is its strong concentration in the capital, Kyiv, where the average monthly income is, at $520, almost double that found in Galicia and thus still 30 per cent higher than the equivalent for Donetsk. A large part of the added value comes from the numerous well-trained IT specialists who, mainly in Kyiv, fulfil orders for Western firms.

The industrialised region of Donbas often claims to be supporting the entire country with its economic output. Looking at it more closely, however, it can be seen that Donbas is actually a net receiver in the internal financial adjustments of Ukraine. Because of the war, the situation has further deteriorated. It will certainly be necessary to consider carefully whether the heavy industry should be reconstructed in its existing form. The events in Donbas may perhaps offer a chance, in the future, for a structural transformation, for instance, on the model of the Ruhr region in Germany.

Generally, Ukraine has shown a rather poor economic performance since the breakdown of the Soviet system. In 1989, Poland and Ukraine started off at a comparable level of economic development; ever since, though, Poland has increased its GDP four times more than Ukraine. While Poland adopted the ambitious Balcerowicz Plan as early as 1989, the first president of independent Ukraine, Leonid Kravchuk (born in 1934), let valuable time elapse by pointing to the alleged lack of economic expertise in Ukraine. His successor, Leonid Kuchma (born in 1938), introduced modest reforms in his first term, after 1994, but became increasingly disappointed with the slow rate of economic development. In his second term, after 1999, he created conditions that were favourable to the rent-seeking practices of a small group of oligarchs. Economic reforms that were promised after the Orange Revolution in

2004 evaporated due to personal squabbles between President Victor Yushchenko and Prime Minister Yulia Tymoshenko. The introduction of a liberalised economy has been hampered ever since by the private business interests of prominent politicians.[1]

The Ukrainian economy is beset by several maladies, maladies that are also familiar in the case of Russia. On the Corruption Perceptions Index of Transparency International, Ukraine in 2018 ranked behind Mali, at 126 out of 183, but still 20 places ahead of Russia. Ukraine's position on the Ease of Doing Business Index of the World Bank looks somewhat better: here Ukraine ranks at 71 on a list of 190 national economies, but it lags considerably behind Russia, which has undertaken important steps towards the reduction of red tape. In Ukraine, only the revolutions of 2004 and 2014 brought about any significant change regarding the transparency of economic policies. The situation remains difficult, and high government positions are still often distributed among business friends. Political financing secures the interests of private stakeholders in governmental decision-making. Petty corruption and small bribes persist, forming a problem in all Ukrainian regions. In 2017, there was an attempt to remove Artem Sytnik, the head of the National Anti-Corruption Bureau, from his office. In 2018, international donors demanded that a High Anti-Corruption Court be set up that would allow measures to be enforced against illegal informal practices.[2] By now, both a National Anti-Corruption Bureau and an Anti-Corruption Court have been set up. Moreover, Ukraine has introduced *ProZorro*, a web tool that enables public monitoring of government procurement. The name is a pun: *prozoro* means 'transparently', and Zorro is famous in popular culture as a fighter for justice.

The sluggish and bloated bureaucracy in Ukraine is also a problem. During his brief period of office in the summer of 2014, the Minister of Economic Development and Trade, Pavlo Sheremeta (born in 1971) attempted to reduce the number of civil servants in his Ministry from 1,200 to 300. He met so much resistance, however, that he abandoned his plan. He was successful merely in reducing the government's fleet of vehicles, which he reduced to 15 per cent of its original level.

Some progress has been made in the case of the taxation system. Before 2004, the tax on corporate profit lay at the confiscatory rate of 30 per cent; but in 2015, a mere 17 per cent was due in tax, and in 2016 it was 16 per cent. Similarly, in 2004, a flat rate was introduced for personal tax that was set at first at the rate of 13 per cent and in the meantime has been raised to 17 per cent. In Ukraine, though, the question must be asked as to whether a flat rate contradicts the fundamental principle of tax justice, in view of the enormous social inequalities in the country. Ukraine still lags far behind when it comes to the administrative effort that remains necessary in order for a tax declaration to be made in accordance with the regulations: in the tax ranking of the World Bank, Ukraine ranked 43rd in 2016. This result represents a dramatic improvement in comparison to 2015, in which Ukraine ended up in 108th position. The leap is mainly due to the introduction of a flat rate of 22 per cent for the Unified Social Contribution tax paid by employers, which replaced previous, considerably higher rates.

The state budget is heavily burdened by pension payments, which, in 2018, made up the most important proportion of the entire budget (occupying about 24 per cent); this is a lot more than the European average, which lies at around 8 per cent. These high commitments derive from the early 2000s, when Yanukovych, who was Prime Minister at the time, was setting out his position for the presidential elections. He greatly extended pension payments in order to expand his voter base. While his calculation did not work out for him in 2004, the resulting inherited pension burden remains to this day.

In the private sector, Western standards of corporate governance are being established, albeit very slowly. Already in 2003, admittedly, the regulator of the Ukrainian Exchange had worked out recommendations, conforming to OECD norms, for the organisation of stock corporations – but in corporate practice, however, many innovations have remained at a quite superficial level. The chair of the supervisory board, who normally is also the owner of the firm, possesses a very strong position as a rule, while by comparison the CEO has few responsibilities. Under such conditions, strategic and operational leadership become mixed up. Checks and balances, moreover, are poorly developed, and it is only in the case of firms with foreign investment that a genuine dialogue takes place between the business management and the supervisory board.[3]

2014, the year of crisis, was a fatal one for the Ukrainian economy. Gross domestic product slumped by 8 per cent; inflation shot up from 1 to 25 per cent; and currency reserves shrank from 16 billion to 7 billion dollars. The Ukrainian currency has also greatly suffered in recent times. After the turn of the millennium, relatively stable conditions prevailed: for years on end, 1 dollar equalled approximately 5 hryvni. Between 2009 and 2013, this rate rose to 8 hryvni; and in February 2014, the National Bank of Ukraine gave up effectively pegging the hryvnia to the dollar. At the beginning of 2015, the price of a dollar was multiplied by a factor of six, by comparison with the level of the previous year, to around 28 hryvni; at least this exchange rate proved to be stable for the following years. Not even the Ukrainian export trade could profit from this collapse in the currency, though, and industrial production in Eastern Ukraine suffered a severe downturn. Many delivery contracts with Russia were cancelled or reduced, which concerned the defence sector above all; and since April 2014, armaments exports to Russia have been forbidden. Since September 2014, Ukrainian foodstuffs have also been subject to Russian import duty.

The trading relations of Ukraine with the EU and with Russia had roughly the same intensity before the dramatic events of 2014, each accounting for 25 per cent of all Ukrainian exports. After the completion of the Association Agreement with the EU, though, Ukrainian foreign trade is being displaced in a westward direction. Out of consideration for Russia, the agreement was not scheduled to come into force until 2016. Already in 2015, Ukrainian exports to Russia dropped to 13 per cent while exports to the EU skyrocketed to 34 per cent. An important prerequisite for the diversification of the national economy was Ukraine's accession to the WTO in 2008. Ukraine is doing everything in its power to reduce its dependency on deliveries of Russian energy. Until the gas crisis in 2009, Ukraine had enjoyed very favourable terms for its Russian gas supply and often paid less than 50 per cent of the global market price.[4] The war with Russia brought a reversal in Ukrainian energy politics. Ukraine stopped buying Russian gas for its own consumption, and turned instead to suppliers from neighbouring EU member states, such as Poland, Slovakia and Hungary. However, this gas may still originate from Russia, taking a detour over Central Europe. A further attempt to solve the problem is unavoidable: the savings potential for natural gas in Ukraine is substantial and has not been exhausted to date, since for a long time the price of gas remained at a low level, meaning that modernisation seemed unattractive to consumers. Because of the annexation of Crimea, furthermore, two ambitious Ukrainian energy projects have come to a premature end. The offshore gas deposits that were discovered in the Black Sea can no longer be exploited; and the plan for an underwater pipeline ('White Stream'), which was supposed to channel Azerbaijani gas into Ukraine via Georgia and Crimea, has also become unrealistic.

The Ukrainian economy urgently needs direct foreign investment. So far, though, investments in Ukraine – compared with the countries in East-Central Europe, but also with Russia – have turned out to be very modest in scale. At the end of 2010, direct investments in Ukraine amounted to around $1,100 per inhabitant. The corresponding figures were, for the Czech Republic, $10,000; for Poland, $4,100; and for Russia, despite everything, $2,000. The absolute total of direct investments in Ukraine reached, at the end of 2008, the level of roughly $35 billion; however, $9 billion of this amount were not really investments but rather tax-privileged backflows of Ukrainian flight capital from Cyprus and the British Virgin Islands.

One great structural problem is represented by the oligarchisation of the Ukrainian economy. In 2014, the assets of the hundred richest Ukrainians amounted to around $42 billion, thus corresponding to just about a third of Ukrainian GDP. One of the central demands of the Euromaidan protest was indeed that the country's riches must be distributed in a more just way. In 2014, however, it was only the accounts of the Yanukovych clan that were frozen; the other oligarchs could freely continue their usual activities, at least domestically. The war has not only badly affected the Ukrainian economy but also led to a meltdown in the assets of the oligarchs. The richest Ukrainian, Rinat Akhmetov (born in 1966), possessed assets amounting to around $16 billion in 2013 – of which he has now lost almost half, in the course of the crisis.

In 2014, the destinies of the oligarchs took very different turns. The fall of Dmytro Firtash (born in 1965) has been the most dramatic; on 12 March

2014, he was arrested at Vienna International Airport. The FBI was looking for him in connection with a bribery affair in which the Russian mafia boss Semion Mogilevich (born in 1946) was also involved. Firtash was released on bail for $125 million, but he was not permitted to leave Austria; and he is still fighting against being extradited to the USA. Traces of Firtash also led to Switzerland until recently: he was substantially involved in the shadowy firm RosUkrEnergo which was domiciled in the tax haven of Zug. The only task of RosUkrEnergo consisted in skimming off profits from the crude oil and natural gas industries. Many attempts to close this trading centre, so prone to corruption, became stuck because the powerful clans of Yushchenko and Yanukovych were participating in the plunder of these profits. The company only ceased to exist around the end of 2014.

Rinat Akhmetov owns numerous steel mills and coal mines in Donbas. He amassed his wealth by means of dubious privatisations. One of the few cases in which these practices became public knowledge concerned the sale of a factory in 2004. The property in question changed hands, without a call for bids, for the sum of $800 million. For once, the authorities became suspicious, and the deal was called off; a year later, an Indian investor bought the factory for six times the former price.[5] At the beginning of the crisis, Akhmetov had been manoeuvring for a long time, wanting to wait until it eventually became clear which side would win the upper hand. Since then he has expressed his loyalty to the government in Kyiv. At the same time, though, Akhmetov has also been securing his home territory. He financed the organisation that succeeded Yanukovych's 'Party of Regions', namely, the so-called 'Opposition Bloc'. At the parliamentary elections in October 2014, this new party achieved a result of 38 per cent in the four easternmost regions of the country, and thus became the strongest political force there. However, even with this success, the 'Opposition Bloc' remained far behind the result in 2012 when the 'Party of Regions' had garnered nearly 70 per cent of the votes cast in Eastern Ukraine. It was thus made clear that, also in Eastern Ukraine, many citizens rejected the corrupt Yanukovych and held his former entourage responsible for the disaster in domestic politics that had taken place in Spring 2014. Akhmetov himself is popular in Donbas because he generously supports the FC Shakhtar Donetsk (currently playing in Kharkiv, because of the conflict), and thus further strengthens the already pronounced self-awareness of the region. Akhmetov's true political stronghold lies in Mariupol. His business interests in this strategically important harbour town on the Sea of Azov are also probably the reason why the separatists have not taken Mariupol, despite several military advances.

Ihor Kolomoyskyi (born in 1963) has experienced a meteoric rise: on 2 March 2014, he was appointed Governor of Dnipropetrovsk. Kolomoyskyi became rich in the banking business in particular. He possesses not just Ukrainian but also Cypriot and Israeli citizenship; and Kolomoyskyi has made no secret of his Jewishness and moreover has become ostentatiously involved in Jewish organisations. The issue of anti-Semitism in Ukraine is still very delicate, and persistent rumours can be heard that Petro Poroshenko and Arseniy Yatsenyuk also come from Jewish families. Together with Poroshenko, Kolomoyskyi supported the Euromaidan protests from the very beginning. In Dnipropetrovsk, Kolomoyskyi offered a bounty of $10,000 for the capture of any separatist. This approach, highly questionable in constitutional terms, secured great sympathy for him among the population. In any case, his policies are efficient: to date, Dnipro has remained unharmed by separatist upheavals. However, after a power game with President Poroshenko, Kolomoyskyi was relieved of his duties as Governor on 25 March 2015. This confrontation also had an economic dimension. Kolomoyskyi's main asset was *Privat Bank*, a credit institution with a powerful network all over Ukraine. In 2016, *Privat Bank* was nationalised against Kolomoyskyi's will. Ever since, he has been struggling to win *Privat Bank* back.

Petro Poroshenko (born in 1965) has often been mocked as the 'Chocolate King'. Nevertheless, his business empire also comprises insurance, sport clubs, shipyards, radio stations and agronomic companies. In May 2014, when he was elected President, he achieved the impressive result of winning 54 per cent of all the votes. Moreover, he was the first Ukrainian president to win the vote in all regions. Poroshenko could profit from the weakness of his most important competitors: in an ill-fated gesture during the Euromaidan negotiations, Vitali Klitschko (born in 1971) shook the hand of Yanukovych and thereby discredited himself in the eyes of the general population; meanwhile, Yulia Tymoshenko (born in 1960) was thought by many Ukrainians to be a power-hungry self-promoter whose infighting with Yushchenko was what had made the rise of Yanukovych possible in the first place. In the presidential election of 2019, Poroshenko made it into the run-off but then lost to the political newcomer Volodymyr Zelensky (born in 1978).

Yulia Tymoshenko has experienced an extremely up-and-down career, both as an oligarch and as a politician. She made her first steps as an entrepreneur by setting up a video rental store in her native Dnipropetrovsk. In the 1990s, she successfully entered the energy business, and was soon nicknamed the 'gas princess'. Her involvement in the lucrative energy sector came at a price, though. She was indicted and arrested several times over alleged irregularities in her management. In the early 2000s, Tymoshenko consciously reinvented her public image. She started to speak exclusively Ukrainian in public, began to wear her hair in a braided crown in order to invoke Ukrainian folklore traditions, and presented herself as a reformer who fought against oligarchic privileges. In 2009, during her tenure as prime minister under President Yushchenko, Tymoshenko cut a controversial gas deal with Moscow. Two years later, she was accused by Ukrainian prosecutors of having exceeded her competences as prime minister in the allegedly overpriced gas contract; and, in 2011, she was sentenced to seven years in prison. This verdict was widely seen as politically motivated, because Tymoshenko had been the main rival of incumbent president Viktor Yanukovych in the presidential election run-up of 2010. On the peak of the 'Revolution of Dignity', Tymoshenko was released from prison and made a dramatic appearance on the Euromaidan. Sitting in a wheelchair because of pains in her back, and without make-up, she claimed she was the future president of Ukraine. At that time, though, she completely over-rated her own position. Her approval rates were in fact at an all-time low, because public opinion held her accountable for the political and economic failures of the wasted years after the Orange Revolution. Tymoshenko learnt her lesson and stopped cultivating the image of herself as an innocent victim. In 2018, she started a new political campaign and presented herself as a successful manager. However, in the presidential elections of 2019 she obtained merely 14 per cent of the votes and ranked third.

The Ukrainian oligarchs know very well by now that the mere accumulation of capital in a society that is being modernised can lead to social tensions. Almost all business leaders have therefore bought a TV channel of their own, turning it into their mouthpiece in each case. Rinat Akhmetov has command over the TV channel Ukraine; Ihor Kolomoyskyi controls 1+1; Dmytro Firtash runs Inter; and Channel 5 belongs to Petro Poroshenko. Victor Pinchuk (born in 1960) has chosen a different strategy: in 2006, he founded the Kyiv School of Economics and the PinchukArtCentre, a museum for contemporary art, in the Ukrainian capital. He also financed the successful free concerts on the Maidan (Independence Square) in Kyiv that Elton John and Paul McCartney gave in 2007 and 2008 respectively.

An embittered struggle rages behind the scenes between the Ukrainian oligarchs for influence and resources. And it is precisely the close ties between business and politics that hinder a swift reform of the country.[6] Attempts to prevent such alliances have turned out to be short-lived. In December 2014, President Poroshenko hired two US-trained specialists for his government. Natalia Jaresko was born in 1965, in Chicago, to Ukrainian immigrant parents. In the 1990s, she worked for the US Embassy in Kyiv. Later on, she helped in allocating foreign direct investments in Ukraine; and from 2014 to 2016, she was Minister of Finance and managed to cut a deal with the International Monetary Fund (IMF) over Ukrainian debts. Aivaras Abromavičius was born in 1976, in Vilnius. He received his education in Estonia and the USA. After having worked for a Swedish investment company, he became Minister of the Economy.

Both Jaresko and Abromavičius received Ukrainian citizenship only shortly before they were appointed as members of Poroshenko's cabinet. They were well accepted as ministers by Ukrainian citizens, because they possessed high credibility in the everlasting fight against corruption and informal networks. However, in the case of Abromavičius, this fight seems to be lost, at least for the time being. In February 2016, he stepped down and voiced his frustration over the slow progress in establishing a corruption-free business culture. He openly blamed oligarch Ihor Kononenko for exercising a secret influence on state-run companies. Kononenko is a close ally of Poroshenko and seems to enjoy the President's protection.

Natalia Jaresko ended her term as Minister of Finance in April 2016 after Arsenii Yatseniuk had resigned as prime minister. She was mentioned as the possible head of a technocratic government, but Poroshenko's close ally Volodymyr Hroisman was eventually elected as Yatseniuk's successor.

Not all advisors of foreign origin, however, enjoy a similar reputation in Ukraine. In 2015, President Poroshenko appointed the former President of Georgia, Mikheil Saakashvili (born in 1967), as Governor of the Odessa region. Saakashvili ruled with a rod of iron and cleansed the police and the customs authorities. Eventually, though, he lost Poroshenko's support and resigned in 2016. At present, Saakashvili, who was stripped of both his Georgian and his Ukrainian citizenship, is acting as a troublemaker and heading a protest movement that demands the impeachment of President Poroshenko.

The situation remains difficult in many ways. One of the most significant problems is the ongoing war in Donbas. According to Poroshenko, the so-called anti-terrorist operation in Eastern Ukraine costs several million dollars per day. Since the outbreak of war in Donbas, considerable state funds have been flowing into the Ministry of Defence, while at the same time urgently needed income from coal and steel exports has disappeared. It is true that, in order to tide it over its budget difficulties, Ukraine has received several loans from the International Monetary Fund, each amounting to around $10 billion, in 2010, 2014 and 2015.[7] These loans must, however, be completely paid back, and they are not anywhere near enough to get the country back on its feet again. Experts estimate that, for a genuine reconstruction of the Ukrainian economy, loans of at least $200 billion will be necessary.

Notes

1 Oleh Havrylyshyn, *The Political Economy of Independent Ukraine: Slow Starts, False Starts, and a Last Chance?* (London, 2017), p. 9.
2 Amanda Paul, 'Ukraine Should Double Down on Reform in 2018', European Policy Centre, 17 January 2018, available at: www.epc.eu/pub_details.php?cat_id=4&pub_id=8207.
3 Anastasia Tserkovnyuk, 'Corporate Governance in the Ukrainian Banking Sector', PhD thesis, University of St Gallen, 2015.
4 Havrylyshyn, *The Political Economy*, pp. 226, 239.
5 Sergii Leshchenko, 'Ukraine's Oligarchs Are Still Calling the Shots', *Foreign Policy*, 14 August 2014, available at: http://foreignpolicy.com/2014/08/14/ukraines-oligarchs-are-still-calling-the-shots/.
6 Oksana Huss, 'The Perpetual Cycle of Political Corruption in Ukraine and Post-Revolutionary Attempts to Break Through It', in *Revolution and War in Contemporary Ukraine: The Challenge of Change*, ed. Olga Bertelsen (Stuttgart, 2017), pp. 317–352.
7 International Monetary Fund, 'Ukraine', available at: www.imf.org/en/Countries/ukr.

10 The European Union as unwilling protector of Ukraine

Ukraine conceives itself to be a European nation, but at the same time it lies in the political, economic and military sphere of influence of its great neighbour, Russia. Since the escalation that took place in Ukraine in February 2014, the EU has been driven into a role that it did not necessarily want to take on at all, namely, the role of becoming the guarantor of Ukrainian independence. The EU took a long time to figure out a Ukraine policy of its own. By 2004, a certain enlargement fatigue had taken hold of the European bureaucracy in Brussels. Ten new members had joined the EU, and two problematic candidates (Bulgaria and Romania) were still standing on the threshold. The prospect of integrating another economically weak and corruption-ridden East European state did not trigger any enthusiastic reaction. It is one of the ironies of history that the EU and Ukraine were closest in their mutual strategies under the pro-Russian president Viktor Yanukovych. The reason for this anomaly may be the scaled-down character of Ukrainian aspirations at the time, which actually suited the unassertive attitude of the EU. The failed EU summit in Vilnius in November 2013 may be considered a turning point, when President Yanukovych refused to add his signature to the European Association Agreement. The representatives of the EU were completely taken aback by these events. The fact that José Manuel Barroso, the President of the European Commission, and Herman van Rompuy, the President of the European Council, believed even during the meeting in Vilnius that they could still reach an agreement with Yanukovych shows how poor the preparation for the summit really was on the part of the EU.

To this day the EU is prevaricating when it comes to the question of Ukraine's prospects for accession.[1] Since 2009, an 'Eastern Partnership' has existed that envisages Ukraine seeking closer ties with the EU; there is controversy, though, as to whether this 'Eastern Partnership' should lead in the longer term to Ukraine becoming a member of the EU or whether the partnership is intended to be a permanent replacement for such an integration.[2] Meanwhile, progress has been made in several instances: Ukraine's Association Agreement with the EU has been active since 2016, and Ukrainian citizens have been able to travel to the EU visa-free since 2017. In these processes of negotiation, an important role is also played by the complex structure of the EU's foreign policies, which to begin with have to arise out of a synthesis, free from contradiction, of the positions of all twenty-eight member states. It is true that, since 2010, there has been a European External Action Service. The member states, however, jealously guard the primacy of their national interests when it comes to formulating their foreign policies. It is indicative that the association of states in the EU does not have a Foreign Minister as such at its disposal but merely a 'High Representative of the Union for Foreign Affairs and Security Policy'. Catherine Ashton (born in 1956) was the first to hold this office; in November 2014, she was replaced by Federica Mogherini (born in 1973). The authority of the High Representative is limited, having hardly any room for manoeuvre in formulating a political position with regard to the Council of member states, and appearing more as a moderator.

In its European policies, Russia has cleverly exploited this peculiarity of the EU. From the Kremlin's perspective, Brussels is not a priority when it comes to choosing a point of contact; and Russia prefers to negotiate individually with each European government. This approach has the advantage of reducing the waste of diplomatic resources through friction. Furthermore, Putin knows very well that individual European countries (and Germany above all) represent important special interests in Russia – interests that they will also push through against other EU member states. By means of this strategy, Moscow aims to drive a wedge into the common foreign policies of the EU and to play off the individual member states against one another.

However, Putin had not reckoned with the shooting down of the Malaysian passenger aircraft over Eastern Ukraine on 17 July 2014. In Europe, this disaster was attributed to the separatists supported by Moscow. In order to shoot down a plane at great altitude, anti-aircraft missiles would have been needed which were probably moved into Eastern Ukraine by Russia. If this is what happened – and there are now numerous pieces of evidence to support such a conclusion – then Russia must bear joint responsibility for the air disaster. On 1 August and 12 September 2014, with unexpected unanimity, the EU imposed far-reaching economic sanctions, which the Kremlin had not predicted. After the annexation of Crimea in March 2014, the EU had in fact restricted itself to applying travel restrictions to individual representatives of the Russian power elite and freezing their bank accounts. These measures had not been too painful for those concerned, since they had enough time to transfer their foreign assets to a safer place.

By now, the current sanctions have affected Russia in a thoroughly painful way, not so much directly but because of their indirect effects. The climate for investments in Russia has become markedly worse, the flight of capital has reached a record level, the rouble has massively lost value, and Russian Government bonds may soon be downgraded to junk status. Russia's misfortune, though, is not necessarily an advantage for Ukraine. The weak rouble threatens to drag the hryvnia into the abyss as well. Russia remains an important trading partner for Ukraine, as before – and so Ukraine is also affected by any economic crisis in Russia.

In January 2015, the EU further intensified its anti-Russian stance. In a resolution on the situation in Ukraine, the European Parliament expressed its 'full solidarity with Ukraine'.[3] The European Council was urged to consider further sanctions against Russia, especially in the fields of nuclear technology and international financial transactions, if Russia did not give up its destabilising policy in the regions controlled by separatists. This resolution opened up a path for further deliveries of European weapons to Ukraine. Moreover, according to the European Parliament, the energy dependency of both the EU and Ukraine on Russia should be reduced. Finally, the Parliament called for a 'communication strategy' by means of which the EU could counter the Russian 'propaganda campaign'.

Consensus in European policies towards Russia is fragile, however. Austria is one weak link in the chain; already in June 2014, thus just three months after the annexation of Crimea, Putin was received with military honours in Vienna. Later both the Austrian Federal Chancellor and the Foreign Minister publicly expressed doubts about the meaningfulness of the sanctions against Russia. An important advocate of better relations with Russia is the co-governing right-wing liberal party of Austria (the FPÖ), which in 2016 concluded an agreement with the 'United Russia' Party. One of the aims of this co-operation consists in the 'education of the young generation in the spirit of patriotism and commitment to a profession'.

In Greece, the election victory of Syriza, the Coalition of the Radical Left, in January 2015, suited Russia especially well. The new Minister for Foreign Affairs, Nikos Kotzias, was considered to be an admirer of Putin and of Aleksandr Dugin, the Eurasian ideologue. Moscow was quick to offer financial assistance to Athens, in case the negotiations with Western lenders should fail.

Hungary has also pulled out of the EU's anti-Russian coalition. In February 2015, Putin arrived in Budapest with much pomp and signed important treaties concerning energy and business. In August 2017, Putin travelled again to Hungary. In February 2016, July 2018 and September 2018, Viktor Orban visited Moscow and held business talks with President Putin.[4]

Italy's strongman, Matteo Salvini, sympathises with Vladimir Putin's authoritarian politics. Between 2014 and 2019, he travelled seven times to Moscow. Following the example of FPÖ, Salvini's *Lega* concluded in 2017 an agreement with the 'United Russia' Party. Salvini has been vocal about the abolition of the European sanctions against Russia. However, in 2019, a scandal surfaced when allegations became public that *Lega* may have received $65 million from obscure Russian sources.

The majority of European states, though, have taken up clearly pro-Ukrainian positions. Yet despite the sympathies for Ukraine of many heads of government in the EU, the prospect of the country's accession to the EU remains on the far horizon. Recent history, it is true, shows clearly that the EU has knowingly accepted new candidates before they have really fulfilled the necessary economic and structural preconditions. The EU has always taken itself to be a community that aims to secure peace and democracy in Europe. This could be seen not only in the controversial acceptance of Bulgaria and Romania into the project of European integration (both in 2007) but also in the cases of Greece (in 1981) and of Spain and Portugal (both in 1986). The dictatorships in Greece, Spain and Portugal had come to an end, and the European Community made use of this window of opportunity in order to integrate these new democracies permanently into a European system of values.

At the moment it does not look as if Ukraine will be able to profit from a similar mechanism. This has to do, first of all, with the size of the country. Ukraine is, in terms of surface area, the largest state whose borders lie completely within Europe. The country has 43 million inhabitants, which corresponds to about 8 per cent of the entire population of the EU. The low per capita gross domestic product is also a weighty problem: while the average in the EU is around $37,000, Ukraine only just manages to reach $4,000. Lastly, there are several warning voices that appear disenchanted because Bulgaria and Romania were accepted into the EU too soon. At the moment of their acceptance, it was the fight against corruption in particular that clearly lost its impetus, since the most significant means of pressing for reform was then no longer effective. The country to suffer from this negative experience, as a result, is now Ukraine.

In any case, even in Spring 2013, the prospect of accession to the EU was certainly not greeted with unanimous enthusiasm in all the various regions of Ukraine. Clear approval of such a scenario could be discerned only in the western half of the country; in the East and in the South, scepticism or indeed refusal prevailed (Figure 10.1).

On the other hand, a different and more surprising picture was revealed by the considerably more cautious question, in the same survey: 'Do you feel European?' In the answers to this question, the opposition between East and West was clearly weakened. Particularly striking here was the fact that Crimea, with its strongly Russian influences, showed the same results as Kyiv, Kharkiv and Ivano-Frankivsk. At the same time, Donetsk, with its strong regional identity, lay at the same level as Volhynia, which was formerly Polish, in responses to this question.

In summer 2014, the new President of the European Commission, Jean-Claude Juncker (born in 1954), ruled out any expansion of the EU in the subsequent five years. In his Political Guidelines, he formulated what his policy would be as follows:

> When it comes to *enlargement*, I fully recognise that this has been an historic success that brought peace and stability to our continent. However, the Union and our citizens now need to digest the addition of 13 Member States in the past ten years. The EU needs to take a break from enlargement so that we can consolidate what has been achieved among the 28. This is why, under my Presidency of the Commission, ongoing negotiations will continue, and notably the Western Balkans will need to keep a European perspective, but *no further enlargement will take place*

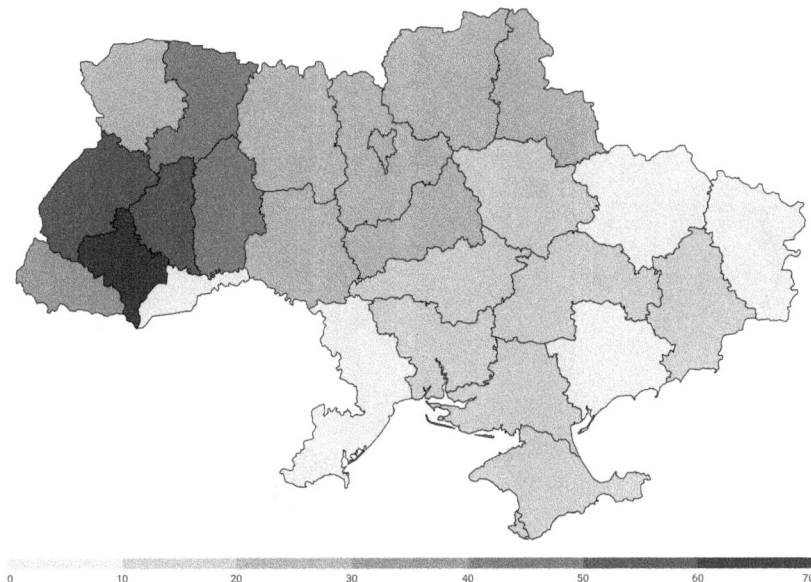

Figure 10.1 Support for EU integration (%)
Source: 2013 survey, available at: www.uaregio.org

over the next five years. With countries in our Eastern neighbourhood such as Moldova or Ukraine, we need to step up close cooperation, association and partnership to further strengthen our economic and political ties.[5]

The EU was driven against its will into solidarity with Ukraine by the dramatic events of 2014. Previously, Russia had been courting Ukraine for a long while. Already in 2011, in an article for the newspaper *Izvestia*, Putin had argued a case for the ambitious project of a Eurasian Union.[6] This Eurasian Union, starting with the creation of a common market, was ultimately supposed to lead to political integration as well, on the model of the European Union. Putin thereby wanted to set up an association of states that in the end would be dominated by Russia and that could deal with the EU on an equal footing; and in 2011 he also announced, grandiosely, that the Eurasian Union would be a reality by 2015. However, since 1 January 2015, there has been merely a 'Eurasian Economic Union', making provisions for a common market between Russia, Belarus, Kazakhstan, Kyrgyzstan and Armenia. The prospect of further integration in a political sense is rather unrealistic. In particular, the President of Kazakhstan, Nursultan Nazarbayev, adopted a much more distant attitude to Russia in the wake of the Russian aggression against Ukraine. In the vote on the United Nations Resolution of 27 March 2014, which demanded that the territorial integrity of Ukraine be maintained,

90 The EU as unwilling protector of Ukraine

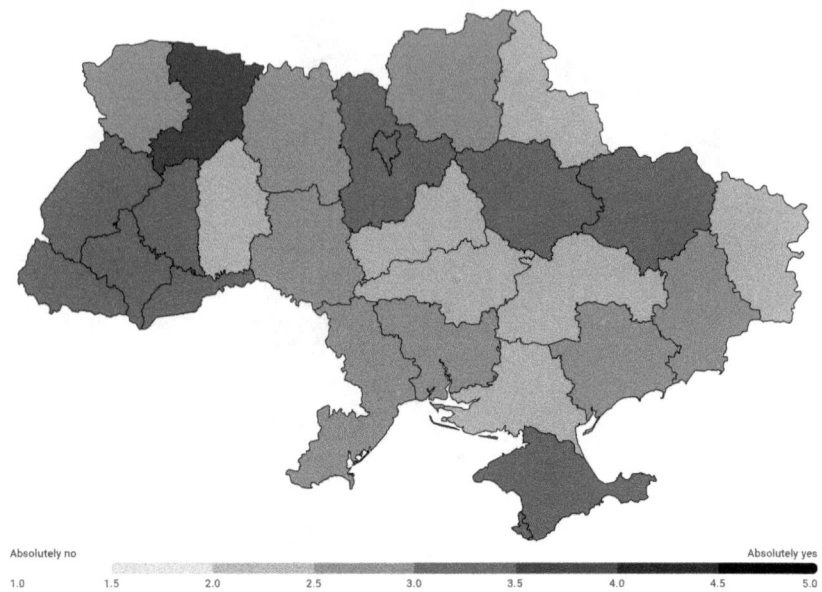

Figure 10.2 Do you feel European? (mean value)
Source: 2013 survey, available at: www.uaregio.org

Kazakhstan turned away from Russia and abstained. After the Russian annexation of Crimea, tension considerably increased in the Kazakh capital, Astana. Around four million ethnic Russians live in Northern Kazakhstan, amounting to about 23 per cent of the population of the entire country. It is only natural that the Kazakh Government fears a scenario emerging for these territories that would be similar to the annexation of Crimea.

After the election victory of Yanukovych in 2010, Putin saw that his great opportunity had come in Ukraine. By means of both carrot and stick, he attempted to win over Ukraine for his project of Eurasian integration and to dissuade the country from forming closer ties with the EU. One important instrument here, for Putin, was the flexible structuring of energy prices for the post-Soviet states. This calculation seems to have worked out in the case of Armenia. In the shadow of the events in Ukraine, the government in Yerevan chose not to sign an Association Agreement with the EU and joined the Eurasian Economic Union instead. In the UN General Assembly, Armenia voted with Belarus, Bolivia, Cuba, Nicaragua, North Korea, Russia, Sudan, Syria, Venezuela and Zimbabwe against the Resolution demanding that the territorial integrity of Ukraine be maintained. In 2017, Armenia and the EU signed a 'Comprehensive and Enhanced Partnership Agreement' (CEPA) that did not conflict with the provisions of the Eurasian Economic Union and was much looser than the EU Association Agreements with Ukraine, Georgia and

Moldova. During the Armenian 'Velvet Revolution' in 2018, both Yerevan and Moscow were eager to declare that there had been no foreign interference in the regime change and that the good relations between the two countries had not been compromised.

The central position that Putin had designated for Ukraine in his Eurasian project is precisely one of the most important reasons for the Kremlin's massive reaction to the events of the Euromaidan. From Moscow's perspective, it was not merely a question of economic issues. Much more important was Russian thinking in geopolitical categories: Ukraine was to have become the cornerstone of the Eurasian Union. At first, everything seemed to indicate victory for Moscow. After the failure of the EU summit in Vilnius, a high-ranking official explained to the newspaper *Vedomosti* that everything had worked out spectacularly well, and the bride had been stolen just before the wedding ceremony.[7] When it then became clear, after the flight of President Yanukovych on 22 February 2014, that Ukraine did not intend to go along with the Russian scenario, alarm bells were set off in Moscow. If Ukraine could not be drawn to the Russian side by means of economic pressures, then the Kremlin wanted to make sure, at least, that the country would not be able to align itself with the West. Therefore, in rapid succession, there followed the concealed military invasion of Crimea, the annexation of the peninsula, the unleashing of armed conflict in Eastern Ukraine and the new staging of a Cold War with the West.

Russia's approach, having contravened international law, means embarking on a path that will allow no turning back. On the other hand, though, the economic, cultural and private links between Ukraine and Russia are so close that it is also not possible simply to demolish all the bridges and to isolate the warring parties from one another. In the years and decades to come, it will be a question of finding a *modus vivendi* that, in pragmatic terms, may permit the countries to live together. Recent developments, however, reveal the deep mistrust remaining between the two nations. Russian TV stations are not allowed to broadcast in Ukraine; Russian books and films with ideological content have been banned from the Ukrainian media market; and direct flight and train connections have been cancelled.

Perhaps Ukraine will be forced to follow the historical example of Finland in its difficult relationship with Russia. After the Winter War of 1939–1940, Finland lost large parts of Karelia to Soviet Russia. Nevertheless, in the years after the war, something like a special relationship was established between Moscow and Helsinki. After the suppression of the Prague Spring in 1968, for instance, the Soviet Premier Alexei Kosygin thus immediately travelled to Helsinki, in order to set out Moscow's view of the situation to the Finnish Government and to offer reassurance that a similar scenario in Finland would be unthinkable.[8] The Government in Kyiv wants to avoid a Finlandisation of its own country at any cost. However, a Ukraine oriented towards Western Europe will also have to come to some sort of arrangement with its enemy, Russia, in the future.

Notes

1. Michael Johns, 'Caught Between Russia and NATO: The EU During and After the Ukrainian Crisis', in *The Return of the Cold War: Ukraine, the West, and Russia*, ed. J. L. Black and Michael Johns (London, 2016).
2. Evhen Tsybulenko and Sergey Pakhomenko, 'The Ukrainian Crisis as a Challenge for the Eastern Partnership', in *Political and Legal Perspectives of the EU Eastern Partnership Policy*, ed. Tanel Kerikmäe and Archil Chochia (Cham, 2016), pp. 167–179.
3. European Parliament Resolution of 15 January 2015 on the Situation in Ukraine, available at: www.europarl.europa.eu/sides/getDoc.do?pubRef=-//EP//NONSGML+TA+P8-TA-2015-0011+0+DOC+PDF+V0//EN.
4. Anton Shekhovtsov, *Russia and the Western Far Right: Tango Noir* (London, 2018).
5. Jean-Claude Juncker, 'A New Start for Europe: My Agenda for Jobs, Growth, Fairness and Democratic Change', Opening Statement in the European Parliament, Strasbourg, 15 July 2014, available at: https://ec.europa.eu/commission/publications/president-junckers-political-guidelines_en. Emphasis in the original.
6. Vladimir Putin, 'The New Integration Project for Eurasia: A Future That Is Born Today', 4 October 2011, available at: http://csef.ru/en/politica-i-geopolitica/223/novyj-integraczionnyj-proekt-dlya-evrazii-budushhee-kotoroe-rozhdaetsya-segodnya-1939.
7. Timothy Heritage and Richard Balmorth, 'Russia Steals "Ukrainian Bride" at the Altar', *Reuters*, 22 November 2013, available at: www.reuters.com/article/us-ukraine-eu-russia/russia-steals-ukrainian-bride-at-the-altar-idUSBRE9AL0UK20131122.
8. Viktor I. Andrijanov, *Kosygin* (Moscow, 2003), pp. 174, 256f.

11 The complicated relationship with the USA and NATO

Diplomatic relations between independent Ukraine and the USA got off completely on the wrong foot. On 1 August 1991, the American President George H. W. Bush (1924–2018) delivered an address to the parliament of what was then still the Ukrainian Soviet Republic. This appearance was termed the 'Chicken Kiev speech' soon afterwards by a renowned *New York Times* columnist. Bush argued against 'suicidal nationalism' and said he favoured a new federal treaty for the Soviet Union, granting more autonomy to member states. The speech was written by Condoleezza Rice (born in 1954), who would later serve as Secretary of State under George W. Bush. The Ukrainian parliament initially welcomed the speech with a standing ovation. In early August 1991, many Ukrainians still held favourable views of the Soviet Union. However, three weeks later, the attempted coup in Moscow that aimed to restore a centralist Soviet government changed the situation completely. Soon, public outrage kicked in. Bush's speech was seen by nationalists as an argument denying full independence to Ukraine. In a referendum held on 1 December 1991, an overwhelming majority (92.3 per cent) of all Ukrainian citizens voted for independence.

The major point of concern for the United States was the presence of nuclear weapons on Ukrainian soil. In the case of Ukraine, the problem was considerable: in 1992, Ukraine possessed the third-largest nuclear arsenal in the world. Ukraine was urged to join the Treaty on the Non-Proliferation of Nuclear Weapons in 1994. In exchange, the United States of America, the Russian Federation and the United Kingdom confirmed in the so-called Budapest Memorandum that they would 'respect the Independence and Sovereignty and the existing borders of Ukraine'. More precisely, the Memorandum stated that all three nuclear powers

> will refrain from the threat or use of force against the territorial integrity or political independence of Ukraine, and that none of their weapons will ever be used against Ukraine except in self-defense or otherwise in accordance with the Charter of the United Nations.

The first two presidents of Ukraine, Leonid Kravchuk (born in 1934) and Leonid Kuchma (born in 1938), did not show any particular interest in a rapprochement with the United States.[1] Relations definitely soured after the Gongadze affair. The journalist Georgiy Gongadze (1969–2000) was kidnapped and brutally murdered in 2000. Gongadze had founded the influential and independent news platform *Ukrainska pravda* and had investigated high-level corruption. Soon after the murder, tape recordings emerged that suggested President Kuchma himself was implicated in Gongadze's murder. Shortly afterwards, Gongadze's widow and her two children were granted political asylum in the United States. In this situation, the White House did everything it could to keep a safe distance from the toxic Ukrainian president. Eventually Kuchma almost became *persona non grata* in the USA. The aversion went so far that US officials insisted that the French spelling of country names be used at a NATO meeting, so that President George W. Bush would not have to sit next to Kuchma.[2]

The Orange Revolution in 2004 came as a relief to the US government. The peaceful protests against the electoral fraud during the presidential elections were backed and supported by several Western non-governmental organisations (NGOs), such as the International Renaissance Foundation, the German Marshall Fund, the US-Ukrainian Foundation, Freedom House, the National Democratic Institute, the Westminster Foundation, the Swedish International Development Cooperation Agency, and grants from Western embassies in Kyiv.[3] This assistance consisted mainly in the training of civic organisations in Ukraine.

The new president, Viktor Yushchenko (born in 1954), sought a close alliance with the United States of America. There were also important private ties. In 1998, Yushchenko had got married for the second time, to US citizen Kateryna Chumachenko, who was born in Chicago and graduated from Georgetown University. During her husband's tenure as prime minister in the early 2000s, Chumachenko was accused by a nationalist Russian journalist of conducting a CIA operation in Ukraine and of exerting undue influence on her husband. In the end, she was naturalised in Ukraine and renounced her US citizenship. Yushchenko had always taken a fiercely anti-Russian stance. The Russian-Georgian war in August 2008 aggravated his aversion against the powerful neighbour even more. As a direct result of this war, the United States and Ukraine signed a Charter on Strategic Partnership on 19 December 2008. The charter explicitly states that both countries should 'support each other's sovereignty, independence, territorial integrity and inviolability of borders'. The document goes on: 'Our friendship comes from mutual understanding and appreciation for the shared belief that democracy is the chief guarantor of security, prosperity and freedom.'[4]

The Euromaidan was greeted with enthusiasm by leading US politicians. In December 2013, Assistant Secretary of State Victoria Nuland visited the Euromaidan. Senator John McCain also travelled to Kyiv and addressed the protesters: 'Ukraine will make Europe better and Europe will make Ukraine better.' After the dramatic turn of events in February 2014, Vice-President Joe Biden and CIA Director John Brennan appeared in Kyiv as well. This prominent American presence was fiercely exploited by Russian propaganda. In state media outlets, these visits were presented as evidence that the events in Ukraine amounted to a CIA-led regime change. Such allegations were, however, quite hypocritical. In February 2014, when events got out of control, Vladislav Surkov, Putin's personal advisor and 'curator of the Ukrainian project', was also present at the Euromaidan.[5]

In 2014, the US Congress passed the Ukraine Freedom Support Act, in a rare display of bipartisan unanimity, which appropriated $350 million in military assistance to Ukraine. While President Obama had been reluctant to deliver lethal weapons to Ukraine, the Trump administration provided the Ukrainian army with anti-tank guided missiles of the Javelin type. In spite of Trump's declared personal sympathies with Putin, the USA clearly sides with Ukraine in the Donbas war. Secretary of Defense James Mattis celebrated Ukrainian Independence Day in Kyiv on 17 August 2017. In his address, he declared:

> Have no doubt, the United States stands with Ukraine. We support you in the face of threats to sovereignty and territorial integrity, to international law, and to the international order. We do not, and we will not, accept Russia's seizure of Crimea and despite Russia's denials, we know they are seeking to redraw international borders by force, undermining the sovereign and free nations of Europe.[6]

In 2017, the Trump administration appointed Kurt Volker as Special Representative for Ukraine. However, Volker's task amounts to mission impossible. He has been lobbying for the deployment of a UN-led peacekeeping force in the Donbas; this proposal, however, has so far met with fierce resistance from Russia. In the course of the Trump-Ukraine controversy, Volker stepped down in September 2019.

Ukraine's relations with the United States have considerable implications for the strategies of safeguarding Ukrainian national security. In 1991, the demise of the communist systems in Eastern Europe also led to the dissolution of the Warsaw Pact. Most East European Countries were eager to join NATO as soon as possible. In four steps (1999, 2004, 2009 and 2017), a belt of new NATO members from Estonia to Montenegro was formed. At the beginning of this enlargement process, NATO considered itself an organisation that wanted to prevent a security vacuum in Eastern Europe and to guarantee the emerging liberal-democratic order in the post-socialist states. In the 1990s, many Western policy-makers did not want to repeat the mistakes that had been made at the conferences in Yalta (February 1945) and Potsdam (July–August 1945), when Churchill and Roosevelt accepted the Soviet zone of influence as proposed by Stalin and thus betrayed the East European states. The main initiative now came, however, from the newly independent states themselves. The evolving position of the Czechoslovakian President Václav Havel is quite representative with regard to many other politicians in this context. In 1990, he had called for a radical change of NATO so that it would include both a revised military doctrine and a new name. Already one year later, he had adopted a much more favourable stance towards NATO.[7] In a speech delivered in March 1991 at NATO Headquarters in Brussels, Havel said:

> From the time when I was young I heard in my country from all official places, as well as from all information media, only one thing about the North Atlantic Alliance: that it was a bastion of imperialism and an incarnation of the Devil himself which threatened peace and wished to destroy us.
>
> I am happy that today I can speak the truth from this rostrum: that the North Atlantic Alliance was, and is, through the will of the democratically elected governments of its member countries, a thoroughly democratic defence association which has made an important contribution to the fact that our continent has not known the troubles of war for almost an entire half-century and that a great part of it has been saved from totalitarianism. If Western Europe enjoys such a degree of democracy and economic prosperity as it does today, it owes this undoubtedly also to the fact that it managed, together with the United States of America and Canada, to create this security alliance as an instrument for the protection of its freedom and of the values of Western civilization.[8]

To be sure, Ukraine had a much more distant relationship to NATO in the 1990s than did Czechoslovakia. However, in 1994, Ukraine was the first post-Soviet country to join the Partnership for Peace programme. In 1999, NATO opened a liaison office in the Ukrainian Ministry of Defence. Officially speaking, Ukraine started its path towards NATO membership in 2002, when the NATO-Ukraine action plan was initiated.

Accession to NATO became a top priority for Ukraine only under President Yushchenko. His efforts culminated in the declaration of the Bucharest NATO summit on 3 April 2008, which affirmed that Ukraine would become a member of NATO. However, support among the Ukrainian populace for NATO membership was rather lukewarm. The Russian aggression in 2014 had a double effect on Ukraine's plans for an accession to NATO. On the one hand, the prospect of NATO membership receded into the distant future; on the other hand, public support for NATO membership increased considerably. In a survey from February 2017, 41 per cent indicated that they would vote for NATO accession, and 32 per cent against. Regional differences are significant, though: in Western Ukraine 65 per cent were in favour of NATO membership, in the centre 41 per cent, in the South 30 per cent, and in the East a mere 15 per cent (Figure 11.1).[9]

Member countries of NATO were also split over Ukraine's ambitions to join. In particular, the USA lobbied for Ukraine, and were backed in doing so by Great Britain, Canada and the new member states from Eastern Europe. Opposition came above all from Germany and France, but also from Italy,

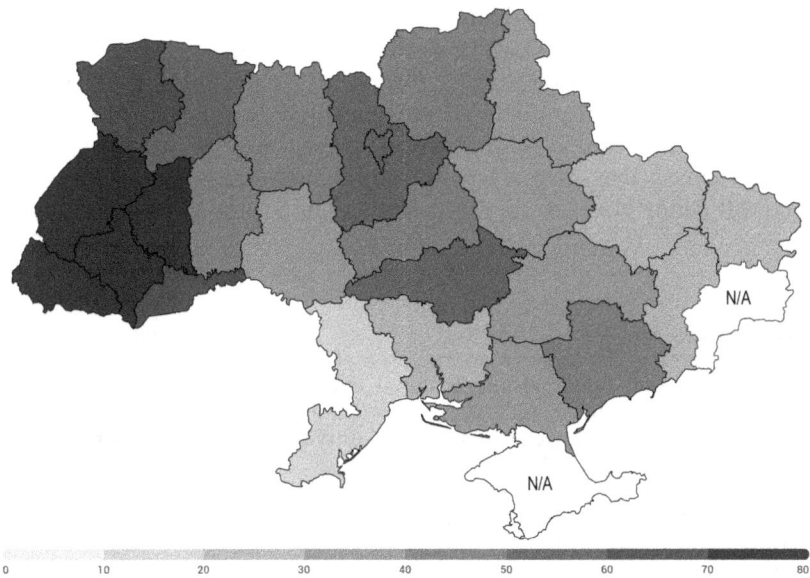

Figure 11.1 Support for Ukraine joining NATO (%)
Source: 2017 survey, available at www.uaregio.org

Spain, Belgium, Luxembourg and the Netherlands. These opponents already feared a Russian backlash and considered the pace of reform in Ukraine to be insufficient. In the following years, the rapprochement between NATO and Ukraine came to a halt. President Yanukovych, who came to power in 2010, did not pursue the accession plans any further; and NATO itself had no consensus over a clear strategy concerning Ukraine's possible membership. Clearly the dispute over Crimea plays into the hands of Russia. While the government in Kyiv claims that Crimea belongs to Ukraine, it admits at the same time that it does not control the entire territory of the state. This, in turn, means that Ukraine does not meet one of the most important accession criteria of NATO. The Russian aggression against Ukraine in 2014 has also affected relations between Russia and NATO. The talks taking place at the Russia-NATO Council were suspended, and resumed only in 2016.[10]

The events of 2014 have raised a crucial question: what security guarantees does a partnership with NATO actually entail? While it is clear that there can be no collective defence action, as provided for in the prominent Article 5 of the NATO Treaty, the Partnership Agreement resembles Article 4 in its wording and provides that the Alliance will 'consult with any active participant in the Partnership if that Partner perceives a direct threat to its territorial integrity, political independence or security'. After the Russian aggression against Ukraine, NATO's reaction was first and foremost rhetorical in nature: Russia's actions were termed a breach of international law and a violation of

Ukraine's sovereignty. Eventually NATO offered Ukraine a Comprehensive Package of Assistance, which includes capacity and institution building, enhancement of C4 (Commands, Control, Communications, Computers), development of an integrated logistics support system, and technical defence co-operation. However, NATO abstained from delivering lethal weaponry to Ukraine, fearing that such a step would intensify the crisis.[11] This cautious stance will define NATO's approach to Ukraine for the foreseeable future.

Notes

1. Taras Kuzio and Paul D'Anieri, *The Sources of Russia's Great Power Politics: Ukraine and the Challenge to the European Order* (Bristol, 2018), p. 76.
2. Michael McFaul, 'Internal and External Factors in Ukraine's 2004 Democratic Breakthrough', in *Democracy and Authoritarianism in the Postcommunist World*, ed. Valerie Bunce, Michael McFaul and Kathryn Stoner-Weiss (Cambridge, 2010), pp. 189–225, pp. 195, 211.
3. Ibid., p. 210.
4. United States-Ukraine Charter on Strategic Partnership, available at: www.state.gov/p/eur/rls/or/142231.htm.
5. Nedim Useinov, 'The Annexation of Crimea: Russia's Response to Ukraine's Revolution', in *Revolution and War in Contemporary Ukraine: The Challenge of Change*, ed. Olga Bertelsen (Stuttgart, 2016), pp. 183–212, p. 187.
6. Secretary of Defense James Mattis, 'Remarks with President Petro Poroshenko, Presidential Palace, Kyiv, Ukraine', available at: www.dod.defense.gov/News/Speeches/Speech-View/Article/1291430/secretary-of-defense-james-mattis-remarks-with-president-petro-poroshenko/.
7. Ronald D. Asmus, *Opening NATO's Door: How the Alliance Remade Itself for a New Era* (New York, 2002), pp. 11, 14.
8. Frank Schimmelfennig, *The EU, NATO and the Integration of Europe: Rules and Rhetoric* (Cambridge, 2003), p. 232.
9. *Ukraine-Analysen* 162, 28 June 2017, p. 22, available at: www.laender-analysen.de/ukraine/pdf/UkraineAnalysen187.pdf.
10. Andrew T. Wolff, 'NATO's Enlargement Policy to Ukraine and Beyond: Prospects and Options', in *NATO's Return to Europe: Engaging Ukraine, Russia, and Beyond*, ed. Rebecca R. Moore and Damon Coletta (Washington, DC, 2017), pp. 71–96, pp. 72–75.
11. Rebecca R. Moore, 'The Purpose of NATO Partnership', in *NATO's Return to Europe: Engaging Ukraine, Russia, and Beyond*, ed. Rebecca R. Moore and Damon Coletta (Washington, DC, 2017), pp. 167–192, pp. 168, 179f.

12 *Quo vadis*, Ukraine?

During the Euromaidan and the subsequent dramatic events on the Crimean peninsula and in Donbas, Ukraine made it into the headlines of Western media on a daily basis. Ever since, the international attention directed towards the situation in Ukraine has diminished considerably. Occasionally, news about violations of the ceasefire break to foreign audiences, but on the whole, Ukraine shares the fate of most long-term conflict areas of the world: that is, it tends to be forgotten.

There are several reasons for this development. First and foremost, the behaviour of the aggressor has changed. Since the middle of 2015, the strategy of the Kremlin no longer focuses on Ukraine. Previously, the war in Ukraine had been exploited in order to rally Russian citizens behind the strong shoulders of their leader, President Putin. However, the Russian Government soon found itself in a discursive dilemma. On the one hand, it boasted of having prevented a bloodbath in Crimea by means of its military intervention. On the other hand, exactly such a tragedy was happening in Donbas, with 2,000 casualties among the civilian population.[1] In this situation it became increasingly difficult to explain to the Russian public why their 'compatriots' in Crimea were being 'saved' while their other 'compatriots', in Donbas, were left behind. The Kremlin chose not to address this obvious problem at all, but rather to divert public attention towards another hotspot in international politics: Syria.

The Russian triumph of the annexation of Crimea was followed by the alleged Russian victory over the international public enemy number one, namely, ISIS. The Kremlin chose a highly symbolic place for its self-congratulatory ceremony: on 4 May 2016, the Orchestra of the Mariinsky Theatre in St Petersburg performed a concert in the Roman amphitheatre of Palmyra. The director of this renowned orchestra, Valery Gergiev, belongs to Putin's circle of over 500 'trusted persons' and has publicly backed the Russian aggression against Ukraine. When the officials responsible for Gergiev's engagement as Director of the Munich Philharmonic asked him to clarify his position, he penned an open letter to his German audience. On 20 May 2014, he wrote:

> I am a musician and a director. But I am also Russian and closely tied to my fatherland ... I cannot turn a blind eye to the fact that Russian

society, to some extent, observes other fundamental principles than those found in Western societies.[2]

Two Russian TV channels broadcast the concert live. Every Russian spectator was able to draw a parallel between the ancient town of Palmyra and the world-famous orchestra from 'the Northern Palmyra', as St Petersburg was called by the Romantic poets of the nineteenth century. The event delivered the following symbolic message: Russian culture prevails over the barbaric terrorism of ISIS, not on foreign soil but on the territory of the cultural roots of Russian imperial power.

One major problem of this communicative strategy is the danger that the Kremlin may fall victim to its own carefully tailored narrative. A case in point was Putin's remark on his annual TV show for Russian citizens, *Direct Line with Vladimir Putin*, on 23 December 2016, when he suggested that it might be time for a reconciliation with Ukraine. This is of course a noble proposal, but Putin is completely delusional about the prospect of a 'normalisation' of the relationship between Russia and Ukraine. Realistically, it may take two or three generations until Russians and Ukrainians will be able sincerely to call each other 'brothers' or 'sisters' again; and to be sure, such a reconciliation must be ruled out during Putin's tenure as President. It is very likely that the situation in Eastern Ukraine will intentionally be stuck in a stalemate. The two fake states around the cities of Donetsk and Luhansk have already turned into a military protectorate of the Kremlin. Their state budgets are augmented by secret cash flows from Moscow. President Putin will do anything to prevent Kyiv from returning these territories to constitutional order.[3] For the Kremlin, there are only two acceptable solutions to the conflict in Eastern Ukraine: either – and this is the more likely outcome – the status quo will be preserved, or a Bosnian-like federation will be established in Ukraine. In the latter case, the 'People's Republics' in Donetsk and Luhansk would be able to veto any further integration of Ukraine into Western economic, political and military structures.

Another reason for the waning international attention directed towards the situation in Ukraine is domestic. The civic mobilisation of the Euromaidan runs the risk of incurring the same fate as the Orange Revolution in 2004. The hopes for a democratic rule of law without corruption, nepotism and bureaucratic inefficiency were dissipated in both cases rather quickly. In the case of the Euromaidan, the costs of the war in Donbas served as a welcome pretext for the Ukrainian Government when it had to explain the slow pace of the reforms. To be sure, there is a considerable amount of truth in this argument, but the ongoing war cannot be held responsible for all the shortcomings in the country's administration. One major problem is Ukraine's electoral system. Half of the 450 Members of Parliament are elected in a proportional voting system with closed party lists, while the other half are elected on the basis of a simple majority system in single mandate districts. The closed party lists provide an excellent opportunity for the parties to sell the best places to the highest-bidding candidates. Without a change to the electoral system, informal power will overshadow the democratic will of the citizens.

A considerable amount of recent legislation has rightfully led to raised eyebrows in the West. On 16 May 2017, President Poroshenko signed a decree banning the Russian equivalents of Facebook, *VKontakte* and *Odnoklassniki*, from Ukrainian cyberspace. The same holds true for access to *Yandex*, a popular Russian search engine. Finally, influential Russian TV channels like ORT, NTV Plus, Zvezda, TNT and REN are also blocked in Ukraine. This decree is only the tip of the iceberg of the cultural war between Russia and Ukraine. Already in 2015, the Ukrainian customs service released a list of 38 Russian books that supposedly propagate 'an ideology of hatred, fascism, xenophobia, and separatism' and threaten 'the territorial integrity and constitutional order of Ukraine'. The list includes works by the far-right ideologue Aleksandr Dugin and the founder of the 'National-Bolshevist' Party, Eduard Limonov. In December 2016, the parliament passed a law prohibiting the import of books that 'create a positive image of aggressor states'. In April 2016, President Poroshenko signed a bill into law that bans all feature films and TV series that were produced in Russia after the annexation of Crimea. The ban also extends to Russian films produced after 1991 if they 'glorify the work of Russian government bodies'. It comes as no surprise, then, that Ukraine ranks only 102nd, out of 180, in the 2019 World Press Freedom Index, compiled by *Reporters without Borders*.

However, the picture in Ukraine is not completely dire. The recession is over. In 2016, the Ukrainian economy returned to growth. The same holds true for the national currency. The hryvnia had been stable for a long time at 8 hryvni to the US dollar, but fell during the crisis to an all-time low of 33 hryvni to the dollar. Now the currency has gained a foothold at 28 hryvni to the dollar. In April 2017, the IMF released a credit note of $1 billion, because the government and the parliament had agreed on a solid budget for the current year. In December 2018, the IMF opened a credit line of $3.9 billion to stabilize the country in the wake of the presidential elections of 2019. The fight against corruption has made some progress: a new law requires public officials to declare their wealth. Moreover, a recently established business ombudsman council deals with complaints from entrepreneurs who are being harassed by the state bureaucracy. Finally, the introduction of visa-free travel to the EU for holders of biometric passports, in the summer of 2017, marks an important success for Ukrainian citizens. Unhindered access to the EU countries was one of the hopes of the participants in the Euromaidan.

The long-term goal behind the visa-free travel, though, namely Ukraine's accession to the EU, seems to have receded into a far distant future. On 15 July 2014, at the peak of the crisis in Donbas, the head of the European Commission, Jean-Claude Juncker, told the EU Parliament that there would not be any enlargement of the EU for the next five years. After this period, furthermore, he opened up the prospect merely for the western Balkan countries. In his speech, he mentioned the partnerships with Ukraine and Moldova but implied that he considered the Association Agreements with these countries as a substitute for, rather than as a first step towards, full EU membership. However, Ukraine remains adamant on this issue. On 7 February 2019, the Ukrainian parliament passed an amendment declaring accession to the EU and NATO to be a constitutional goal.

The most serious problem in Ukraine is the persistence of oligarchic structures in politics, the economy and the public sphere. Former President Poroshenko never divested himself of his private businesses, as he had promised to do before his election. The historian Yaroslav Hrytsak had even warned of the possibility of a 'sweet counterrevolution', alluding to Poroshenko's chocolate industries.[4] Poroshenko was indeed a very versatile politician; he served as a minister under both President Yushchenko and President Yanukovych. His political career was based on a secret deal with opposition leader Vitali Klitschko, who agreed to run for mayor of the city of Kyiv and thus cleared the way for Poroshenko to become president. Ukrainian civil society is capable of considerable efforts, and will take action if need be – as both the Orange Revolution in 2004 and the 'Revolution of Dignity' in 2013–2014 have shown. However, there is a danger that the interactive relationship between state and society will not last and will be replaced by a depoliticised population. In this case, Ukrainian citizens would degenerate into voiceless subjects who do not care about the political decision-making process which, in their eyes, follows its own informal rules anyway.

It is unclear what the result of the presidential election of May 2019 will mean for Ukrainian society. The entire political establishment was challenged by Volodymyr Zelensky, a TV comedian without any experience of public office. Zelensky became famous as the protagonist of the popular TV series *The Servant of the People* that has been on air since 2015. Zelensky plays the role of a modest history teacher, Holoborodko, who accidentally ascends to the position of Ukrainian president. Of course, the topic of the show is not incidental to the 2019 result: in effect, many Ukrainian citizens cast their vote in favour of the fictional character Holoborodko and not the real candidate. Zelensky exploited the symbolic capital of his TV show even further by creating a party with the same name, *The Servant of the People*. In his electoral campaign, Zelensky successfully pursued a catch-all strategy. He carefully avoided any precise political agenda, and vaguely promised to fight corruption, to boost the economy and to end the war. His followers form a very heterogeneous, even self-contradictory group: 56 per cent are in favour of joining NATO, while 35 per cent want to remain non-aligned; 55 per cent call for greater distance to Russia, while 32 per cent wish to re-establish good relations; 52 per cent support Ukrainian as the exclusive state language, while 41 per cent claim that all languages should have the same status; 47 per cent advocate market capitalism, while 41 per cent opt for a state-controlled economy.[5] Zelensky managed to attract the sympathies of all voters who, for whatever reason, were unhappy with the current situation in Ukraine. He explicitly stated in a public debate with Poroshenko: 'I am not your opponent, I am your verdict!' Zelensky's frequent use of the Russian language earned him the respect of many Ukrainian citizens who feel disenfranchised by the dominance of the official state language. On the other hand, for this very reason Zelensky is considered by many Ukrainian intellectuals to be an unreliable patriot, sometimes even an asset of the Kremlin. However, in time for the election Zelensky managed to surround himself with serious experts such as the former Minister of the Economy, Aivaras Abromavičius. Moreover, he enjoys the financial and media support of the exiled oligarch Ihor Kolomoyskyi – to such a degree that some commentators call him the oligarch's stalking horse. Nevertheless, Zelensky won the presidential elections in the run-off against Poroshenko with a landslide victory: 73 per cent of all votes cast.

As of now, Ukraine seems to have achieved a condition that was called, in Communist Poland of the 1960s, the 'little stabilisation'. At the time, this notion meant that Polish society was categorically against the larger framework of its political organisation but had also agreed to accept it for the time being. It took Poland twenty-five years to become an independent and democratic nation state that could even eventually opt for questionable political choices of its own. It is very much possible that, twenty-five years from now, Ukraine will also be a prosperous nation state with a colourful historical past and a common future that is based on a civic consensus about social justice and good governance.

Notes

1 Office of the United Nations High Commissioner for Human Rights, 'Accountability for Killings in Ukraine from January 2014 to May 2016', 25 May 2016, available at: www.ohchr.org/Doc<ments/Countries/UA/OHCHRThematicReportUkraineJan2014-May2016_EN.pdf.
2 Valery Gergiev, Letter to subscribers and supporters of the Munich Philharmonic, May 2014, available at: www.merkur.de/bilder/2014/05/20/3571488/1984911777-brief-valery-gergiev.pdf.
3 Rajan Menon and Eugene Rumer, *Conflict in Ukraine: The Unwinding of the Post-Cold War Order* (Cambridge, MA, 2015), p. 86.
4 Yaroslav Hrytsak, 'Sladkaia kontrrevolutsiia', *Novoe vremia*, 5 August 2017, available at: http://nv.ua/opinion/grytsak/sladkaja-kontrrevoljutsija-1607641.html.
5 See 15 politychnykh dilem: Shcho proponuiut kandydaty v prezydenty ta obiraiut ikh prykhyl'nyky. Razumkov Tsentr, 19 March 2019, available at: www.razumkov.org.ua/images/Material_Conference/2019_03_19/2019_Prezent_ukrinform.pdf.

Appendix: List of historical city names

Berdychiv
: city in Zhytomyr region; before 1793 (Polish-Lithuanian Commonwealth) Berdyczów (Polish); 1793–1917 (Russian Empire) Berdichev (Russian); 1917–1920 (Ukrainian People's Republic); 1920–1991 (Soviet Ukraine); since 1991 (Ukraine) Berdychiv (Ukrainian); other name - באַרדיטשעוו [Bardichev] (Yiddish).

Brody
: city in Lviv region; before 1772 (Polish-Lithuanian Commonwealth) and 1919–1939 (Second Polish Republic) Brody (Polish); 1772–1918 (Austrian Empire) Brody (German); 1918–1919 (West Ukrainian People's Republic), 1939–1941; 1944–1991 (Soviet Ukraine); since 1991 (Ukraine) Brody (Ukrainian); other names: בראָד [Brod] (Yiddish), Brody (Russian).

Chełm
: city in eastern Poland; before 1387 (Kievan Rus, Kingdom of Galicia-Volhynia); 1387–1795 (Polish-Lithuanian Commonwealth); 1795–1815 (Austrian Empire); 1815–1917 (Russian Empire) Kholm (Russian); 1917–1918 (Ukrainian People's Republic) Хёлм [Holm] (Ukrainian); 1918–1939 (Second Polish Republic); 1939–1944 (German Occupation) Kulm (German); 1944–1989 (Polish People's Republic); since 1989 (Polish Republic) Chełm (Polish); other name: כעלם [Khelm] (Yiddish).

Chernivtsi
: administrative centre of Chernivtsi region; before 1774 (Principality of Moldavia); 1774–1918 (Austrian Empire) Czernowitz (German); 1918 (West Ukrainian People's Republic); 1918–1940 (Romania) Cernăuți (Romanian); 1940–1941 (Soviet Ukraine); 1941–1944 (Romania) Cernăuți (Romanian), 1944–1991 (Soviet Ukraine); since 1991 (Ukraine) Chernivtsi (Ukrainian); other names:

Appendix: List of historical city names 105

	טשערנאָוויץ [Tshernovits] (Yiddish), Czerniowce (Polish), Chernovtsy (Russian).
Chortkiv	city in Ternopil region; 1522–1772 (Polish-Lithuanian Commonwealth); 1772–1918 (Austrian Empire); 1918–1919 (West Ukrainian People's Republic); 1919–1939 (Second Polish Republic) Czortków (Polish); 1939–1940 (Soviet Ukraine); 1941–1944 (German Occupation) Tschortkau (German); 1944–1991 (Soviet Ukraine); since 1991 (Ukraine) Chortkiv (Ukrainian); other names: טשאָרטקאָוו [Chortkov] (Yiddish), Chortkov (Russian).
Dnipro	administrative centre of Dnipropetrovsk region; before 1797 (Russian Empire) Yekaterinoslav (Russian); 1797–1802 (Russian Empire) Novorossiysk (Russian); 1802–1918 (Russian Empire); 1918–1926 (Ukrainian People's Republic/Soviet Ukraine) Katerynoslav/Yekaterinoslav (Ukrainian/Russian); 1926–1991 (Soviet Ukraine); 1942–1943 (German Occupation) Dnepropetrowsk (German); 1991 (Ukraine) Dnipropetrovsk (Ukrainian); since 2016 Dnipro (Ukrainian), other names: Dnepropetrovsk and Dnepro (Russian).
Donetsk	administrative centre of Donetsk region; 1869–1924 (Russian Empire and Soviet Ukraine) Yuzivka/Yuzovka (Ukrainian/Russian); 1924–1929 (Soviet Ukraine) Stalin (Ukrainian); 1929–1961 Stalino (Ukrainian); 1942–1943 (German Occupation) Donezk (German); 1961–1991 (Soviet Ukraine); since 1991 (Ukraine) Donetsk (Ukrainian/Russian).
Ilovaisk	city in Khartsyzk municipality, Donetsk region.
Ivano-Frankivsk	administrative centre of Ivano-Frankivsk region; 1662–1772 (Polish-Lithuanian Commonwealth) Stanisławów (Polish); 1772–1809 (Austrian Empire); 1809–1815 (Russian Empire) Stanislav (Russian); 1815–1918 (Austrian Empire); 1918–1919 (West Ukrainian People's Republic) Stanyslaviv (Ukrainian); 1919–1939 (Second Polish Republic); 1939–1941 (Soviet Ukraine); 1941–1944 (German Occupation) Stanislau (German); 1944–1962 (Soviet Ukraine) Stanislav (Ukrainian); 1962–1991 (Soviet Ukraine); since 1991 (Ukraine) Ivano-Frankivsk (Ukrainian); other names: סטאַניסלאַוו [Stanislav] (Yiddish), Ivano-Frankovsk (Russian).

106 Appendix: List of historical city names

Izmail	city in Odessa region; before 1812 (Danubian Principalities/Ottoman Empire), 1812–1856 (Russian Empire) Tuchkov (Russian); 1856–1878 (Danubian Principalities/Ottoman Empire); 1878–1917 (Russian Empire) Ismail (Russian); 1918–1940 (Romania) Ismail or Smil (Romanian); 1940–1941 (Soviet Ukraine); 1941–1944 (Romania) Ismail or Smil (Romanian); 1944–1991 (Soviet Ukraine); since 1991 (Ukraine) Izmail (Ukrainian); other names: Ismail (Bulgarian), Ismajil (German), İşmasıl or Hacidar (Turkish).
Kamianets-Podilskyi	city in Khmelnytsk region; before 1352 (Kievan Rus) Kamianets (Old Slavonic); 1352–1672 (Polish-Lithuanian Commonwealth); 1672–1699 (Ottoman Empire) Kamaniçe (Turkish); 1699–1793 (Polish-Lithuanian Commonwealth); 1793–1917 (Russian Empire) Kamieniec Podolskiy; 1917–1919 (Ukrainian People's Republic); 1919–1920 (Second Polish Republic) Kamieniec Podolski (Polish); 1920–1941(Soviet Ukraine); 1941–1944 (German Occupation) Kamjanez-Podilskyj (German); 1944–1991 (Soviet Ukraine); since 1991 (Ukraine) Kamianets-Podilskyi (Ukrainian); other name: קאמענעץ־פאדאלסק [Kamenets-Podilsk] (Yiddish).
Kerch	city in the Crimean Autonomous Republic of Ukraine occupied by the Russian Federation; seventh century BC–sixth century AD (Greek colony, Kingdom of Bosporus, Kingdom of Pontus) Panticapaeum (Ancient Greek); sixth–seventh centuries (Byzantine Empire) Bospor (Ancient Greek); seventh–tenth centuries (Khazar Khaganate) Karcha (Turkic); tenth–thirteenth centuries (Kievan Rus); thirteenth–fourteenth centuries (Mongol Empire) Korchev (Old Slavonic); 1318–1475 (Genoese colony) Cerco (Italian); 1475–1774 (Crimean Khanate under the suzerainty of the Ottoman Empire) Keriç/Kerç (Crimean Tatar/Turkish); 1774–1917 (Russian Empire); 1918–1954 (Soviet Russia) Kierch (Russian); 1954–1991 (Soviet Ukraine); since 1991 (Ukraine) Kerch (Ukrainian).
Kharkiv	administrative centre of Kharkiv region; 1654–1917 (Tsardom of Russia, Russian Empire); 1918 (Ukrainian People's Republic); 1919–1991 (Soviet

Appendix: List of historical city names 107

	Ukraine); 1941–1943 (German Occupation) Charkow (German); since 1991 (Ukraine) Kharkiv/Kharkov (Ukrainian/Russian).
Kherson	administrative centre of Kherson region; 1778–1917 (Russian Empire) Kherson (Russian); 1918–1919 (Ukrainian People's Republic); 1919–1991 (Soviet Ukraine); 1941–1944 (German Occupation) Cherson (German); since 1991 (Ukraine) Kherson (Ukrainian).
Kolomyia	city in Ivano-Frankivsk region; 1240–1340 (Principality of Halych-Volhynia) Kolomyia (Old Slavonic); 1340–1498 (Polish-Lithuanian Commonwealth); 1498–1531 (Principality of Moldavia) Colomeea (Romanian); 1531–1772 (Polish-Lithuanian Commonwealth); 1772–1918 (Austrian and Austro-Hungarian Empire); 1918–1919 (West Ukrainian People's Republic); 1919–1939 (Second Polish Republic) Kołomyja (Polish); 1939–1941 (Soviet Ukraine); 1941–1944 (German Occupation) Kolomea (German); 1944–1991 (Soviet Ukraine); since 1991 (Ukraine) Kolomyia (Ukrainian); other names: קאָלאָמײ [Kolomej] (Yiddish), Kolomyia (Russian).
Košice	city in eastern Slovakia; 1230–1804 (Kingdom of Hungary); 1804–1918 (Austrian and Austro-Hungarian Empire); 1918–1938 (Polish-Lithuanian Commonwealth); 1938–1945 (Kingdom of Hungary) Cassa, Cassovia, Kassa (Hungarian); 1945–1992 (Czechoslovakia); since 1993 (Slovakia) Košice (Slovak); other names: Kaşa (Turkish), Kaschau (German), קאַשוי [Kashoy] (Yiddish).
Kropyvnytsky	administrative centre of Kirovohrad region; before 1917 (Russian Empire) Elisavetgrad (Russian); 1917–1924 (Ukrainian People's Republic, Soviet Ukraine) Elyzavetgrad (Ukrainian); 1924–1934 (Soviet Ukraine) Zinovyevsk (Ukrainian); 1934–1939 (Soviet Ukraine) Kirovo (Ukrainian); 1936–1991 (Soviet Ukraine); since 1991 (Ukraine) Kirovograd (Ukrainian), since 2016 Kropyvnytsky.
Kryvyi Rih	1775–1917 (Russian Empire); 1918 (Donetsk–Krivoy Rog Soviet Republic) Krivoy Rog; 1918–1919 (Ukrainian People's Republic); 1919–1991 (Soviet Ukraine); 1941–1944 (German Occupation) Kriwoi Rog (German); since 1991 (Ukraine) Kryvyi Rih (Ukrainian).

Kyiv	capital of Ukraine; 882–1363 (Kievan Rus); 1363–1569 (Grand Duchy of Lithuania) Kyjevŭ, Kyiv, Kiev (Old Slavonic); 1569–1649 (Polish-Lithuanian Commonwealth) Kijów (Polish); 1649–1654 (Cossack Hetmanate); 1654–1917 (Tsarsdom of Russia and Russian Empire) Kiev (Russian); 1917–1921 (Ukrainian People's Republic); 1921–1991 (Soviet Ukraine); 1941–1943 (German Occupation) Kiew (German); since 1991 (Ukraine) Kyiv (Ukraine).
Luhansk	administrative centre of Luhansk region; 1795–1917 (Russian Empire); 1918 (Donetsk–Krivoy Rog Soviet Republic); 1919–1935 (Soviet Ukraine) Lugansk (Russian); 1935–1942 (Soviet Ukraine) Voroshylovhrad (Ukrainian); 1942–1943 (German Occupation); 1943–1958 (Soviet Ukraine) Voroshylovhrad (Ukrainian); 1958–1970 (Soviet Ukraine); 1970–1990 (Soviet Ukraine) Voroshylovhrad (Ukrainian); 1990–1991 (Soviet Ukraine); since 1991 (Ukraine) Luhansk (Ukrainian).
Lviv	administrative centre of Lviv region; 1256–1349 Lviv (Old Slavonic); 1349–1772 (Kingdom of Poland, Polish-Lithuanian Commonwealth); 1772–1918 (Austrian and Austro-Hungarian Empire); 1918–1919 (West Ukrainian People's Republic); 1919–1939 (Second Polish Republic) Lwów (Polish); 1939–1941 (Soviet Ukraine); 1941–1944 (German Occupation) Lemberg (German); 1944–1991 (Soviet Ukraine); since 1991 (Ukraine) Lviv (Ukrainian); other names: Leopolis (Latin), לעמבערג/לעמבעריק, [Lemberg/Lèmberik] (Yiddish), Lvov (Russian).
Mykolaiv	administrative centre of Mykolaiv region; 1789–1917 (Russian Empire) Nikolaev (Russian); 1919 (contested territory); 1920–1991 (Soviet Ukraine); 1941–1944 (German Occupation) Nikolajew (German); since 1991 (Ukraine) Mykolaiv (Ukrainian).
Odessa (Odesa)	administrative centre of Odessa region; 1794–1917 (Russian Empire); 1917–1920 (contested territory); 1920–1991 (Soviet Ukraine); 1941–1944 (German Occupation); since 1991 (Ukraine) Odessa/Odesa (Russian/Ukrainian); other names: אדעס [Odes] (Yiddish), Hacıbey (Turkish).
Pereiaslav-Khmelnytskyi	city in Kyiv region; tenth–fourteenth centuries (Kievan Rus, Grand Duchy of Lithuania)

Appendix: List of historical city names 109

Pereyaslav-Ruskyi, Pereyaslav (Old Slavonic); 1569–1648 (Polish-Lithuanian Commonwealth) Perejasław (Polish); 1648–1654 (Cossack Hetmanate); 1654–1917 (Tsardom of Russia, Russian Empire); 1917–1920 (Ukrainian People's Republic); 1920–1941 (Soviet Ukraine) Pereyaslav (Ukrainian/ Russian); 1941–1943 (German Occupation) Perejaslaw (German); 1943–1991 (Soviet Ukraine); since 1991 (Ukraine) Pereiaslav-Khmelnytskyi (Ukrainian).

Poltava administrative centre of Poltava region; ninth century–1569 (Kievan Rus, Grand Duchy of Lithuania); 1569–1648 (Polish-Lithuanian Commonwealth); 1648–1654 (Cossack Hetmanate); 1654–1917 (Tsardom of Russia, Russian Empire); 1917–1920 (Ukrainian People's Republic); 1920–1941 (Soviet Ukraine) Poltava (Ukrainian/Russian); 1941–1943 (German Occupation) Poltawa (German); 1943–1991 (Soviet Ukraine) Poltava (Ukrainian/Russian); since 1991 (Ukraine) Poltava (Ukrainian).

Rakhiv city in Transcarpathia; fifteenth–sixteenth centuries (Kingdom of Hungary); sixteenth–seventeenth centuries (Principatul Transilvaniei under the suzerainty of the Ottoman Empire) Rahó/Rahău (Hungarian/Romanian); seventeenth century–1918 (Austrian and Austro-Hungarian Empire) Rahó/ Rauhau (Hungarian/German); 1918–1919 (Hutsul Republic); 1919–1939 (Czechoslovakia) Rachov (Slovak); 1939–1944 (Kingdom of Hungary) Rahó (Hungarian); 1944–1991 (Soviet Ukraine); since 1991 (Ukraine) Rakhiv (Ukrainian); other names: Rakhovo (Rusyn), ראחוב [Rakhev] (Yiddish), Rakhov (Russian).

Sevastopol city in the Crimean Autonomous Republic of Ukraine occupied by the Russian Federation; 1783–1917 (Russian Empire); 1920–1942 (Soviet Russia) Sievastopol (Russian); 1942–1944 (German Occupation) Sewastopol (German); 1943–1954 (Soviet Russia) Sievastopol (Russian); 1954–1991 (Soviet Ukraine); since 1991 (Ukraine) Sevastopol (Ukrainian); other name: Aqyar (Crimean Tatar).

Simferopol administrative centre of the Crimean Autonomous Republic of Ukraine occupied by the Russian

	Federation; seventeenth century–1784 (Crimean Khanate under the suzerainty of the Ottoman Empire) Aqmescit (Crimean Tatar); 1784–1917 (Russian Empire); 1918 (Soviet Ukraine); 1919–1954 (Soviet Russia) Simferopol (Russia); 1941–1944 (German Occupation) Simferopol (German); 1954–1991 (Soviet Ukraine); since 1991 (Ukraine) Simferopol (Ukrainian).
Ternopil	administrative centre of Ternopil region; 1540–1772 (Kingdom of Poland, Polish-Lithuanian Commonwealth) Tarnopol (Polish); 1772–1918 (Austrian and Austro-Hungarian Empire); 1918–1919 (West Ukrainian People's Republic); 1919–1939 (Second Polish Republic); 1939–1941 (Soviet Ukraine); 1941–1944 (German Occupation) Tarnopol (German); 1944–1991 (Soviet Ukraine); since 1991 (Ukraine) Ternopil (Ukrainian); other names: טארנאָפּל/טערנעפּאָל [Ternepol/Tarnopl] (Yiddish), Ternopol (Russian).
Uzhhorod	administrative centre of Transcarpathia; 895–1804 (Principality of Hungary, Kingdom of Hungary); 1804–1918 (Austrian and Austro-Hungarian Empire); 1919–1938 (Czechoslovakia) Užhorod (Czech/Slovak); 1938–1944 (Kingdom of Hungary) Ungvar (Hungarian); 1944–1991 (Soviet Ukraine); since 1991 (Ukraine) Uzhhorod (Ukrainian); other name: אונגוויר [Ungwir] (Yiddish).
Vyzhnytsia	city in Chernivtsi region; before 1774 (Principality of Moldavia under the suzerainty of the Ottoman Empire); 1774–1918 (Austrian Empire) Wischnitza or Wiznitz (German); 1918 (West Ukrainian People's Republic); 1918–1940 (Romania) Vijniţa (Romanian); 1940–1941 (Soviet Ukraine); 1941–1944 (Romania) Vijnţa (Romanian); 1944–1991 (Soviet Ukraine); since 1991 (Ukraine) Vyzhnytsia (Ukrainian); other names: וויזשניץ [Vizhnitz] (Yiddish), Wyżnica (Polish), Vizhnitsa (Russian).
Yalta	city in the Crimean Autonomous Republic of Ukraine occupied by the Russian Federation; before 1475 (Genoese colony) Etalita or Galita; 1475–1783 Crimean Khanate (Crimean Khanate under the suzerainty of the Ottoman Empire) Yalta (Crimean Tatar); 1783–1917 (Russian Empire); 1919–1954 (Soviet Russia) Yalta (Russian); 1941–1944 (German Occupation) Jalta

Appendix: List of historical city names 111

Zaporizhia	(German); 1954–1991 (Soviet Ukraine); since 1991 (Ukraine) Yalta (Ukrainian). administrative centre of Zaporizhia region; 1770–1806 (Russian Empire) Aleksandrovskaya; 1806–1921 (Russian Empire, Soviet Ukraine) Alexandrovsk; 1917–1918 (Ukrainian People's Republic) Oleksandrivsk (Ukrainian); 1921–1991 (Soviet Ukraine); 1941–1943 (German Occupation) Saporoshje (German); since 1991 (Ukraine) Zaporizhia (Ukrainian).

Bibliography

Anne Applebaum, *Red Famine: Stalin's War on Ukraine* (New York, 2017).
Kate Brown, *A Biography of No Place: From Ethnic Borderland to Soviet Heartland* (Cambridge, MA, 2004).
George G. Grabowicz, *Toward a History of Ukrainian Literature* (Cambridge, MA, 1981).
Henry E. Hale and Robert W. Orttung (eds), *Beyond the Euromaidan: Comparative Perspectives on Advancing Reform in Ukraine* (Stanford, CA, 2016).
Olexiy Haran and Maksym Yakovlyev (eds), *Constructing a Political Nation: Changes in the Attitudes of Ukrainians during the War in the Donbas* (Kyiv, 2017).
Oleh Havrylyshyn, *The Political Economy of Independent Ukraine: Slow Starts, False Starts, and a Last Chance?* (London, 2017).
Paul Robert Magocsi, *A History of Ukraine* (Washington, DC, 1996).
Mikhail Minakov, *Development and Dystopia: Studies in Post-Soviet Ukraine and Eastern Europe* (Stuttgart, 2018).
Serhii Plokhy, *The Gates of Europe: A History of Ukraine* (New York, 2015).
Serhii Plokhy, *Chernobyl: The History of a Nuclear Catastrophe* (New York, 2018).
Ivan L. Rudnytsky, *Essays in Modern Ukrainian History*, ed. Peter L. Rudnytsky (Edmonton, 1987).
Ulrich Schmid and Oksana Myshlovska (eds), *Regionalism Without Regions: Reconceptualizing Ukraine's Heterogeneity* (Budapest, 2019).
Marci Shore, *The Ukrainian Night: An Intimate History of Revolution* (New Haven, CT, 2018).
Orest Subtelny, *Ukraine: A History* (Toronto, 1988).
Andrew Wilson, *Ukraine Crisis: What It Means for the West* (New Haven, CT, 2014).
Serhy Yekelchyk, *Ukraine: Birth of a Modern Nation* (Oxford, 2007).
Larissa M. L. Zaleska Onyshkevych and Maria G. Rewakowicz (eds), *Contemporary Ukraine on the Cultural Map of Europe* (Abingdon, 2009).
Tatiana Zhurzhenko, *Borderlands into Bordered Lands: Geopolitics of Identity in Post-Soviet Ukraine* (Stuttgart, 2010).

Index

Abkhazia 68
Abromavičius, Aivaras 83, 103
Adorno, Theodor W. 37, 40n12
Adventis Church 13
Aeneid (Virgil) 19
Akhmetov, Rinat 51–2, 80, 81, 83
Tsar Alexander II 22
Alwart, Jenny 67n25
Andorra 59
Andrijanov, Viktor I. 92n8
Andrukhovych, Yurii 34, 35, 39n2
Annales School in France 3
Antonovych, Volodymyr 31n13
Armeyskov, Sergey 31n23
Applebaum, Anne 66n3
Argentina 59
Armenia 89; 'Velvet Revolution' in (2018) 91
Aschheim, Steven E. 67n15
Ashton, Catherine 86
Ashton, E.B. 40n12
Asmus, Ronald D. 98n7
Ausländer, Rose 36–7, 40n9–11
Australia 59
Austrian Ukraine 32–3; writers'; invocation of 33–4
Austro-Prussian War 32
Autocephalous Orthodox Church 13, 14

Babi Yar, massacre of Kyvian Jews at 60
Bachmann, Ingeborg 37
Bachynsky, Yulian 33–4
Balmorth, Richard 92n7
Bandera, Stepan 45, 62–3
Baptist Church 13
Barroso, José Manuel 85

Patriarch Bartholomew of Constantinople 15
Battle of Warsaw (Jerzy Hoffman film) 44
Bavaria 2
Becker, Douglas 76n5
Belarus 53, 89
Belgium 9
Belinsky, Vissarion 20–21
Berdyansk 74
Berdychiv 104; mass killings of Ukrainian Jews in 60
Beria, Lavrenti 52–3
Berlin Academy of Music 51
Besters-Dilger, Juliane 17n6
Biden, Joe 94–5
Bilensky, Serhiy 31n13
bilingualism 9
Bismarck, Otto von 3
The Black Council (Kulish, P.) 21–2
Bollack, Jean 40n13
Bowring, Bill 16n4
Brecht, Bertolt 28
Breedlove, General Philip M. 72
Brennan, John 94–5
Brest, Church Union of (1596) 42, 51
Brest-Litovsk Agreement (1918) 24
Brezhnev, Leonid 26
Brockhaus and Efron Encyclopedic Dictionary 22
Brodsky, Joseph 27, 31n23
Brody 104
Bryullov, Karl 20
Budapest Memorandum 93
Bukovina 32, 35, 38, 49; historical perspective 50–51; Sovietisation of 62
Bulgaria 88
Bunce, Valerie 98n2

Index

Burg, Josef 38–9, 40n16
Bush, George H. W. 93
Bush, George W. 93–4
Byron, George Gordon, Lord Byron 28

Canada 28, 59
Carpatho-Rusyn people 50
The Castle of Kaniów (Seweryn Goszczyński poem) 42
Catalonia, separatist tendencies in 54
Catherine the Great 23, 65–6, 71
Celan, Paul 35, 36, 37, 40n8
Charles XII of Sweden 29
Chelm 53, 104
Chernivtsi (formerly Czernowitz) 2, 32, 35–8, 49, 51, 104–5; literary heritage of 35–9; 'Little Vienna' of imperial age 39; Meridian literary festival in 35
Chernomyrdin, Viktor 29
China 29
Chochia, Archil 92n2
Chortkiv 105
Chumachenko, Kateryna 94
Church Union of Brest (1596) 15
Churchill, Winston S. 95
Coletta, Damon 98n11
Colombia 59
Cosmopolitanism and the National State (Meinecke, F.) 61
Council of Europe 12
Crimea 16, 27; annexation of (2014) 30, 68, 69, 90, 99–100; Autonomous Republic of 55; bridge to Russian mainland, construction of 74; crisis in 99; historical perspective 52; Krushchev's policies concerning 53–4; language spoken in 12
Crimean Tatars 53, 54, 75
Crimean War (1853–1856) 52
Saints Cyril and Methodius, Brotherhood of 20
Czech Republic 2, 80
Czechoslovakia 2, 4, 6, 50

D'Abernon, Viscount Edgar Vincent 44, 47n3
D'Anieri, Paul 98n1
'Death Fugue' (Paul Celan poem) 37
Debaltseve 73
The Deluge (Sienkiewicz, H.) 43
Dickinson, Emily 37
Direct Line with Vladimir Putin (TV programme) 71, 100
Dnieper River 6, 23, 41, 54

Dnipro 51–2, 105; Holocaust Museum in 60
Dnipropetrovsk 65–6, 81–2
Don Juan of Kolomyia (Sacher-Masoch, L. von) 35
Donbas 4, 6, 8; historical perspective 51–2; industrialised region of 77; Russian assault on (and crisis in) 30, 50, 68–9, 73, 74, 84, 99
Donetsk (formerly Yuzovka) 8, 51–2, 53, 73, 76, 77, 88, 105; language spoken in 12; People's Republic of Donetsk 4, 6, 15, 17n10
Donetsk-Krivoy Rog 55
Donskoy, Grand Prince Dmitry 19
Dontsov, Dmytro 60–62, 67n11, 67n13, 67n16–18
Dovbush, Oleksa (Carpathian brigand) 35
Dovzhenko, Alexander 25
Drahomanov, Mykhailo 23–4, 31n13, 60, 61
Dugin, Aleksandr 87, 101
The Duma about Waclaw (Zaleski, J.B.) 42
The Dunka of Hetman Kosiński (Zaleski, J.B.) 42
Dzerzhinsky, Felix 63
Dziuba, Ivan M. 63, 67n20

Ecuador 59
Ekaterinoslav 65–6
Ems Decree (1876) 22
Eneyida (Ivan Kotliarevsky play) 19
Metropolitan Epifaniy (Serhii Dumenko) 14–15
Estonia 53
Euromaidan protests in Kyiv 5–6, 14, 54, 63, 66, 80, 82–3, 91, 94–5, 99, 100, 101
European Union (EU) 29, 41, 69, 73, 74; Association Agreements with Ukraine, Georgia and Moldova 90–91; 'Comprehensive and Enhanced Partnership Agreement' (CEPA) 90–91; trading relations between Ukraine and 79–80; Ukraine and, relationship between 85–9, 102

Patriarch Filaret of Kyiv Patriarchate 14–15
Finland, Russia and, relationship between 91
The Fire (Friedrich, J.) 59
Fire in the Steppe (Sienkiewicz, H.) 43

Index 115

First World War 24, 32
Firtash, Dmytro 80–81, 83
Flanders, separatist tendencies in 54
For the Right (Franzos, K.E.) 35
Forbes magazine 27
Förster-Nietzsche, Elisabeth 61, 67n14
France, Symbolism in 37
Franko, Ivan 33, 35
Emperor Franz Joseph I of Austria 32, 34
Franzos, Karl Emil 35
Frederick the Great of Prussia 61
Freedom House 94
Friedrich, Jörg 59, 67n8

Gaidai, Oleksandra 67n21
Galicia 2, 8, 32–3, 34–5, 41, 44; Austrian *Rast* of 24; confrontation between Poles and Ukrainians in 43; cradle of Ukrainian nationalism 49–50; German invasion of (1939) 45–6; Greek Catholic Church in 13, 14, 15; Organisation of Ukrainian Nationalists (OUN) in 45; Polish loss of 49–50; Sovietisation of 62; 'West Ukrainian People's Republic' in 50, 55
Gast, Peter 61, 67n14
Gazprom 29
Georgia 68, 69, 90
Gerasimov, General Valerii 69, 76n4
Gergiev, Valery 99–100, 103n2
German Democratic Republic 53
Germany 9; *Anschluss* against Austria 38; federalism in 55; history of ideas in 3; Nazi Germany, massacres perpetrated by 60; Romanticism in 37; Weimar Republic in 61
Giedroyc, Jerzy 44, 47
Girkin, Igor ('Strelkov') 71
Goethe, Johann Wolfgang von 9, 16n2
Gogol, Nikolai 19–20, 30n6, 31n7
Goll, Ivan 37
Golts, Alexander 76n3
Gongadze, Georgiy (and 'Gongadze affair') 5, 94
Goszczyński, Seweryn 42
Grabowicz, George 30n5
Graziosi, Andrea 67n6
The Great Exodus (Guido Knopp TV series) 59
Greece 88; Syriza election victory in 87
Greek-Catholic Church in Galicia 13, 14, 15, 42

Grossman, Vassily 60
Grucza, Franciszek 39n5

Habsburg Empire 24, 32–3; collapse of 43; internal hierarchy of peoples under 33
Hagen, Mark von 7n3
The Haidamak (Sacher-Masoch, L. von) 35
Hans Küchelgarten (Nikolai Gogol verse epic) 19
Hašek, Jaroslav 7n2
Havel, Václav 95–6
Havrylyshyn, Oleh 84n1, 84n4
Herder, Johann Gottfried von 21, 31n12
Heritage, Timothy 92n7
History of the Ukraine-Rus (Hrushevsky, M.) 2–3
Hitler, Adolf 25, 28, 29, 37, 38, 45; power, seizure of (1933) 61–2
Hódosi, Eszter Kocsisné 7n1
Hoffman, Jerzy 44
Höhne, Steffen 39n5
Hollande, François 73
Holocaust 39, 60
Holodomor (great famine) 57–8, 58–60
Hom, Stephanie Malia 16n3
Hroisman, Volodymyr 84
Hromada (journal) 23
Hrushevsky, Mykhailo 2–3, 7n4, 16, 24
Hryshko, Vasyl 57, 66n2
Hrytsak, Yaroslav 7n8, 16, 17n11, 66n1, 102, 103n4
Hungary 2, 12, 80, 87
Huntington, Samuel P. 4, 7n6
Huss, Oksana 84n6

Ilovaisk in Ivano-Frankivsk 105; embattled small town of 73
Independent Ukraine (Mikhnovsky manifesto) 24
International Criminal Court 68
International Monetary Fund (IMF) 83, 84, 84n7, 101
International Renaissance Foundation 94
Internationalism or Russification? (Dziuba, I.) 63
'Into Life' (Rose Ausländer poem) 36
Italy 9, 87
Ivano-Frankivsk 88
Izmail 49, 106
Izvestia (newspaper) 89
'In Jail' (Rose Ausländer poem) 36

Janion, Maria 47n2
Japan 29
Jarábik, Balázs 56n11
Jaresko, Natalia 83–4
The Jews of Barnow (Franzos, K.E.) 35
John, Elton 83
Johns, Michael 92n1
Joris, Pierre 40n8
Józewski, Henryk 45
Juncker, Jean-Claude 88–9, 92n5, 101–2

Kaganovich, Lazar 57–8, 67n5
Kakanian culture 34
Kamianets-Podilskyi 106; mass killings of Ukrainian Jews in 60
Karunyk, Kateryna 17n6
Kas'ianov, Georgiy 17n11, 67n10
Kazakhstan 89–90
Keller, Gottfried 28
Kerch 106
Kerch Strait 74
Kerikmäe, Tanel 92n2
Kerski, Basil 47n6, 48n10
Kharkiv 24, 70, 81, 88, 106–7; Holocaust Museum in 60; LOT flights to 41; mass killings of Ukrainian Jews in 60
Kherson 71, 107
Khmelnytsky, Bohdan (Cossack Hetman) 23
Khrushchev, Nikita 26, 52–3
Khvylovy, Mykola 26
Kirovohrad 65–6
Klimt, Gustav 34
Klitschko, Vitali 82, 102
Knopp, Guido 59
Kobylianska, Olha 36
Kobzar (Taras Shevchenko poems) 66
Kocsis, Károly 7n1
Kolomoyskyi, Ihor 52, 81–2, 83, 103
Kolomyia 107
Koropeckyj, Roman 31n8
Košice, Slovakia 1, 107
Kostomarov, Nikolay 20–21, 31n13, 60–61
Kosygin, Alexei 91
Kotliarevsky, Ivan 19, 30n4
Kotzias, Nikos 87
Kouchner, Bernard 69
Kovbasiuk, Alla 66–7n4
Kravchuk, Leonid 77, 93–4
Kravtsova, Yekaterina 76n2
Kremer, Arndt 16n2
Kropyvnytsky 107
Kryvyi Rih 107

Kubijovyc, Volodymyr 47n5
Kuchma, Leonid 5, 28, 31n25, 46, 56n4; economic reforms of 77–8; Gongadze affair and 93–4
Kulish, Mykola 26
Kulish, Panteleimon 20–22, 31n14, 60–61
Kulyk, Volodymyr 17n7–8
Kurbas, Les 26
Kuzio, Taras 31n22, 98n1
Kwaśniewski, Aleksander 41
Kyiv (Kiev) 4, 5, 24, 25, 70, 77, 108; Euromaidan protests in 5–6, 14, 54, 63, 66, 80, 82–3, 91, 94–5, 99, 100, 101; language spoken in 12; LOT flights to 41; Orange Revolution and demonstrations in 28
Kyiv Patriarchate of Ukrainian Orthodox Church 13, 14–15
Kyivan Rus 18–19, 22
Kyrgyzstan 89

Lang, Kai-Olaf 47n6
Lenartowicz, Joanna 47n4
Lenin, Vladimir Ilyich 25, 63
Leshchenko, Sergii 84n5
Levchuk, Nataliia 66–7n4
Liber, George O. 31n20
Liebich, Andre 67n19
Limonov, Eduard 101
Lithuania 2, 53
Lombardy 34
Luckyj, George S. N. 31n9
Luhansk 4, 6, 70, 73, 108; language spoken in 12
Lviv 8, 25, 32, 49, 50, 108; defence by Polish schoolchildren and students (*Orlęta Lwowskie*) of (1918–19) 43; LOT flights to 41; mass killings of Ukrainian Jews in 60; murder of school superintendent in (1926) 45

McCain, John 94
McCartney, Paul 83
McFaul, Michael 98n2
Magocsi, Paul Robert 31n15, 50, 56n3
Magris, Claudio 34, 39n1
Makarska, Renata 47n6, 48n10
Malaysian flight MH17, shooting down of 72–3
Malczewski, Antoni 42
Mal'gin, Andrej 56n5
Mallarmé, Stéphane 37
The Man Without Qualities (Museil, R.) 39n4

Index   117

Mandelstam, Osip 37
Maria: A Ukrainian Story in Verse (Antoni Malczewski) 42
Mariupol 74, 81
Marshall Fund 94
Marty, Anton 32
Masaryk, Tomáš Garrigue 50
Matthew, Gospel of 20
Mattis, James 95, 98n6
May, Markus 40n14
Mazepa, Hetman Ivan 28–9
Me (Khvylovy, M.) 26
Medvedev, Dmitry 56n7, 59
Meerbaum-Eisinger, Selma 37–8, 40n15
Meinecke, Friedrich 61, 67n12
Mennonite Church 13
Menon, Rajan 103n3
Merkel, Angela 73
Metahistory (White, H.) 3
Meyer, Ronald 30n6
Mickiewicz, Adam 33
Mijnssen, Ivo 31n27
Mikhnovsky, Mykola 15, 24, 31n18
Minsk Protocol (September, 2014) and Minsk II Agreement 73–4
Mogherini, Federica 86
Mogilevich, Semion 81
Moldova 68, 89, 90
Montinari, Mazzino 67n14
Moore, Rebecca R. 98n11
Mormon Church 13
Moscow Patriarchate of Ukrainian Orthodox Church 13, 14
Moscow Times 68–9
Musil, Robert 39n4
Musiyenko, Oleksiy 57
Mussolini, Benito 61
Mykolaiv 108
Myshlovska, Oksana 17n6, 17n9, 67n19

Napoleon Buonaparte 3
nation states, national culture and 8–9
National Democratic Institute 94
Nationalism (Dontsov, D.) 60
Navalny, Alexei 6
Nazarbayev, Nursultan 89
New York Times 93
Tsar Nicholas II 24
Nietzsche, Friedrich 61
Non-Proliferation of Nuclear Weapons, Treaty on (1994) 93
Nord Stream 29
North Atlantic Treaty Organization (NATO) 30, 69, 74, 94; Bucharest Summit (2008) 18; Comprehensive Package of Assistance for Ukraine from 98; Ukrainian national security and 95–8, 102
Novgorod, medieval principality of 19
Nuland, Victoria 94

Obama, Barack 95
Odessa (Odesa) 24, 70, 108; Holocaust Museum in 60; LOT flights to 41; mass killings of Ukrainian Jews in 60
Odnoklassniki 101
Olpińska, Magdalena 39n5
One Could Make Several Stories from This (Prokhasko, T.) 35
'Operation Vistula' (1947) 46
Orange Revolution (2004) 5, 8–9, 28, 41, 47, 59, 94, 100, 102; economic reforms promised after 77–8
Orban, Viktor 87
Organisation for Security and Co-operation in Europe (OSCE) 73
'Organisation of Ukrainian Nationalists' (OUN) 60, 62, 64–5
Orzechowski, Stanisław 42
Osadchuk, Bohdan 47, 48n10
Osnova (journal) 21
Crown Prince Otto Habsburg 35

Pakhomenko, Sergey 92n2
'Party of Regions' 52, 55, 81
Paul, Amanda 84n2
Pavlovsky, Gleb 68–9
Pereiaslav-Khmelnytskyi 108–9
Pereyaslav agreement (1654) 23, 53
Petliura, Symon 24–5, 43, 45, 50, 57
Petrovsky, Grigory 66
Outlines of a Philosophy of the History of Man (Herder, J.G.) 21
Pidmohylny, Valerian 26
Pieracki, Bronisław 45, 62
Pike, Burton 39n4
Piłsudski, Józef 25, 43–4, 45, 58
Pinchuk, Victor 83
Plokhy, Serhii 47n1, 66–7n4
Plotnitsky, Igor 73
Podgorny, Nikolai 26
Podolia 41
'Poem' (Selma Meerbaum-Eisinger) 37–8
A Poet of Betrayal (Ivan Franko pamphlet) 33
Poland 2, 6, 80; Balcerowicz Plan in (1989) 77; coup in (May, 2926) 44; January uprising in (1863) 22; loss of

Galicia 49–50; Nazi occupation of 62; People's Republic of 46–7; Russian partition of (1830) 22; *Rzeczpospolita* (Commonwealth) of 22, 41–2, 43; Second Polish Republic 43–4, 46, 47; Ukraine and, relationship between 41–7
Polonisation 15, 32, 34, 42, 44–5
Poltava 109; Battle of (1709) 28, 29
Ponomaryov, Vyacheslav 12, 71
Pop-Eleches, Grigore 56n9
Poroshenko, Petro 14, 15, 52, 63–4, 73; economics in Ukraine and 82, 83–4; future prospects for Ukraine 101, 102, 103
Portnov, Andrei 48n8, 56n2, 67n22
Portugal 88
Potemkin, Prince Grigory 66, 71
Potsdam Conference (1945) 95
Privat Bank credit institution 82
Prokhasko, Taras 35
Protestantism 13
ProZorro web tool on government procurement 78
Prymak, Thomas Michael 31n10
Pushkin, Alexander 19–20, 27, 28; statue in Kharkiv of 24
Putin, Vladimir 5, 6–7, 18, 30n1, 63; charm offensive on Ukraine (2007) 28–9; 'Eurasian Union,' promotion of 29; European Union (EU), Ukraine and 86–7, 89, 92n6; future for Ukraine and 99, 100; national independence for Ukraine and 52, 54; Trump and, relationship between 95; Ukraine crisis 68–74, 76n6–7, 76n10

The Radetzky March (Roth, J.) 35
The Rainbow (Rose Ausländer poems) 36
Rakhiv 2, 109
Razumkov Tsentr 103n5
Read, Christopher 67n7
Red Army 33, 38, 53, 62, 63
Red Star (Soviet Army newspaper) 60
Rehn, Olli 69
Reisinger, Heidi 76n3
Reporters without Borders 101
'Revolution of Dignity' (2013–2014) 102
Riabchuk, Mykola 8, 16n1, 28, 31n26, 56n1
Rice, Condoleezza 93
Rilke, Rainer Maria 34
Robertson, Graeme 56n9
Roman Catholicism 13, 14
Romanchuk, Robert 31n8
Romania 2, 9, 12, 37, 38, 49, 88
Rompuy, Herman van 85
Roosevelt, Franklin D. 95
RosUkrEnergo 81
Roth, Joseph 35, 39n6
Rudnytsky, Ivan L. 31n17
Rudnytskyi, Omelian 66–7n4
Rukh civil rights movement 81
Rumer, Eugene 103n3
Ruska Besida, emergence of 51
Russia 12; Acmeism in 37; aggression in Ukraine, effects of 63–6; caesaropapism of Russian Orthodoxy 15; capital flight from 6; Christianisation of (988) 18; Cossack Hetmanate 23; Crimea, annexation of (2014) 30, 68, 69, 90, 99–100; Crimean crisis, perspective on 4; development of (1990s) 4–5; Donbas, assault on (2014) 30; European Union (EU) sanctions on 86–7; Finland and, relationship between 91; Georgia, *Blitzkrieg* on (2008) 29; historiography of 18; Kyivan Rus 18–19, 22; military power, loss of effectiveness of 74; Novorossiya ('New Russia'), concept of 71–2; October Revolution (1917) 24; 'plausible deniability,' diplomacy of 72; Poland, Russian partition of (1830) 22; Polish-Ukrainian pact against Bolshevism in 43–4; propaganda, mobilisation of (2014) 70–71; recognition of Ukrainian as separate language (1905) 22; 'reverse asymmetrical warfare' in Ukraine by 29–30; Russian Federation (RF) 68–9, 69–70; state symbolism of 18; territorial claims, historical legitimations of 54; Ukraine and, importance of relationship between 29–30; Ukraine and, international law and relationship between 91; Ukraine and, 300th anniversary of 'reunification' of (1954) 23; Ukrainian-language publications forbidden in 32–3; Ukrainian 'schismatics,' condemnation of 14; Ukrainian separatism, concerns about 21–2; undeclared war in Ukraine 69–70; warfare style, performance of intimidating manoeuvres in 72; White Russia (Belarus) 23
Russia Calling (investment forum) 72

Index 119

Russia One TV 70
Russian-Georgian war (2008) 94
Ruthenians 33, 42, 51

Saakashvili, Mikheil 84
Sacher-Masoch, Leopold von 35
Sachsenhausen concentration camp 62
Salvini, Matteo 87
Sasse, Gwendolyn 56n8
Savel'ev, Yurii 56n6
Schengen border 41
Schiller, Friedrich 9, 16n2
Schimmelfennig, Frank 98n8
Schmid, Ulrich 17n6, 17n9, 48n9
Schmidt, Josef 51
Schmidt, Knud Rahbek 30n3
Schumpeter, Joseph 32
Schwenk, Hans-Jörg 39n5
Scotland, separatist tendencies in 54
Sea of Azov, Russian control of 74
The Second Polish-Ukrainian War (Viatrovych, V.) 46
Second World War 37, 45–6, 51, 53, 54, 64; Ukrainian Insurgent Army (UPA) in 60, 62, 64–5
Serebrennikov, Artem 31n23
Sereda, Ostap 39n7
The Servant of the People (TV series) 102
Sevastopol 27, 109
Shakhtar Donetsk FC 81
Shcherbytsky, Volodymyr 26
Shchors (Alexander Dovzhenko film) 25
Shekhovtsov, Anton 92n4
Shelest, Petro 26
Sheremeta, Pavlo 78
Shevchenko, Taras 20–21, 22, 27, 35, 66, 67n24
Shevchuk, Pavlo 66–7n4
Sholokhov, Mikhail 58
Shtepa, Pavlo 57
Shukhevych, Roman 62
Shumsky, Alexander 26
Sienkiewicz, Henryk 43, 44
Simferopol 109–10; mass killings of Ukrainian Jews in 60
Simonek, Stefan 34, 39n3
Skoropadskyi, Hetman Pavlo 24
Skrypnyk, Mykola 26
Slezkine, Yuri 31n19
Slovakia 2, 59, 80
Sloviansk 71
Słowo Polskie (newspaper) 45
Smarzowski, Wojciech 46–7
Snyder, Timothy 29, 31n29

Sobiński, Stanisław 45
Solzhenitsyn, Alexander 27, 31n24
South Ossetia 68
Soviet Union: collapse of 49; federation of Soviet republics, project for 27; *korenizatsiya* (putting down roots policy of) 25–6; NKVD in 36; Perestroika in 54; political repression and brutality in Ukraine 26; power hierarchy in 52–3; Russian hegemony in 28; Soviet Federative Socialist Republic (RSFSR) 54; transferal of Crimea to Ukraine (1954) 52, 53; Ukraine in era of, tragedies of 57–66; Ukrainian culture, promotion of 26–7
Spain 9, 88
Spanish Civil War 38
Stalin, Joseph 2, 3, 25–7, 50, 52–3, 67n5, 95; agricultural policy (1932–1933) 57–8; preference for Russian people among Soviets 58–9
Stalingrad, Battle of 29, 62
'Stanislav phenomenon' 33
Stoner-Weiss, Kathryn 98n2
Surkov, Vladislav 95
Surzhyk (Ukrainian-Russian hybrid language) 9
Sweden 41; International Development Cooperation Agency 94
Switzerland 9, 55
Swoboda, Victor 31n11
Sytnik, Artem 78

Tagliavini, Heidi 73
Ternopil 110
Ther, Philipp 17n11
Tillett, Lowell 31n21
Titushko, Vadym (and 'Titushki') 5
Toal, Gerard 31n27, 76n8
Transcarpathia 2, 49; regional self-awareness in 50
Transnistria 68
Transparency International 78
Transylvania 34
Trotsky, Leon 53
Trudeau, Pierre 28
Trump, Donald 95
Tsarist Empire 22, 25, 44; collapse of 24
Tserkovnyuk, Anastasia 84n2
Tsipko, Maria 70
Tsybulenko, Evhen 92n2
Turchynov, Oleksandr 12
Turk Stream 29
Tuscany 34

120 Index

Twelve Rings (Andrukhovych, Y.) 35
Tymoshenko, Yulia 5, 13, 78, 82–3

UEFA European Championship 75
Ukraine: academic research on 2–3; anti-semitism in, issue of 81–2; Association Agreement with European Union (EU) 41; autonomy claims for, Russian surprise at 27; boundary between East and West and, Dontsov's perspective on 61–2; breadbasket of Russia 77; civil society in, development of 5; Constitution of 1996 in 55; Corruption Perceptions Index (Transparency International) 78; Crimean crisis, perspective on 4; crisis for (2014–2018) 68–76; cultural history and traditions of 4; currency restabilisation 101; decentralisation and reform in 56; development of (1990s) 4–5; direct foreign investment, need for 80; division of, proposals for Czech model 6; Ease of Doing Business Index (World Bank) 78; East-West split in 8; East-West split in, language and religion in opposition 15–16; economy of 77–84; energy politics 80; energy supplies for and through, Russia and 29; federalization in, debates about 55–6; geography and demographics 8–16; geopolitical courting by Russia of 29; Greater Russian cultural imperialism and 27–8; gross domestic product (GDP) slump (2014) 79; heterogeneous state 54; hromadas in 56; international attention on situation in, waning nature of 100–101; Kyivian Rus and, factional differences between 18–19; languages in, distribution of use of 12–13; linguistic situation in 9; literature of, modern beginnings of 19–21; 'little stabilisation' in, achievement of 103; map of inter-war years 3; memories, Holomodor and politics of 60; national consciousness 50; National Guard 70; national independence for (1991) 49–50; nationhood for, assertion of 21–2, 23–4; nineteenth century map 33; oligarchisation of economy 80–81, 83; pension payments in state budget 79; Poland and, relationship between 41–7; political strife in, language problem and 9–12; precarious situation in 6–7; private sector corporate governance 79; regions of 49; religious confessions in, complex nature of 13–14; Russia and, importance of relationship between 29–30; Russia and, 300th anniversary of 'reunification' of (1954) 23; Russian aggression in, effects of 63–6, 74–5; Russian TV channels blocked in 101; Russian undeclared war in 69–70; Sobornist unity (January 1919) in 25; social closeness of Ukrainians in face of Russian aggression 75–6; Soviet era in, tragedies of 57–66; Soviet political repression and brutality in 26; taxation system 78–9; territorial integrity of, UN resolution on (March 27, 2014) 89–90; territorial plans of Bachynsky for 33–4; trading relations between EU and 79–80; transferal of Crimea to (1954) 52, 53; 'Ukrainian People's Republic' (UNR), attempted establishment of 24–5, 63; Ukrainian-Russian brotherhood 27; Ukrainian Cossack myth 23; Victory Day (May 9th) in 65; visa-free travel, long-term goal of 101–2

Ukraine: The Birth of a Nation (Jerzy Hoffman documentary film) 44
O Ukraine, Our Soviet Land (Shelest, P.) 26
Ukraine-Analysen 98n9
'Does Ukraine Have a History?' (Von Hagen, M.) 2
Ukraine Is Not Russia (Kuchma, L.) 28
'Ukraine Without Jews' (Vassily Grossman Report, 1943) 60
Ukrainian Cossacks 43, 53
'On Ukrainian Independence' (Joseph Brodsky poem) 27
Ukrainian Institute of National Remembrance 65
Ukrainian Insurgent Army (UPA) 46, 60
Survey of Ukrainian Literature (Kulish, P.) 21
Ukrainian Nazi battalions and SS division 'Galicia' 62
Ukrainian Orthodox Church 13–14
Ukrainian People's Republic 43–4, 49
Ukrainian Regionalism: Research Platform 17n5, 17n12

Ukrainian-Russian hybrid language ('Surzhyk') 9
Ukrainian Soviet Republic 2; foundation of 25–6
Ukrainska pravda 94
Ulbricht, Justus H. 39n5
United Nations (UN): Charter of 93; Resolution (March 27, 2014) 89–90
United States 29; Charter on Strategic Partnership with Ukraine 94; diplomatic relations between independent Ukraine and 93–5; federalism in 55; Holodomor, political recognition in 59; Ukraine Freedom Support Act (2014) 95; US-Ukrainian Foundation 94
Useinov, Nedim 98n5
Ustryalov, Nikolay Vasilyevich 58
Uzbekistan 54
Uzhhorod (formerly Ungvár) 1–3, 49, 110; history 2; inhabitants 2; intersection of four countries near 2; journey from Košice to 1

Vakulenko, Serhii 17n6
Valuyev, Pyotr 22
Vedomosti (newspaper) 91
Venice Commission 12
Viatrovych, Volodymyr 46, 48n7
Viking (Andrei Kravchuk film) 19
Virgil 19
VKontakte 101
Vladimir-Suzdal, medieval principality of 19
Vladimir the Great, Prince of Kievan Rus 18–19, 52
Volhynia and 'Volhynia Experiment' 25, 41, 45, 46–7, 62, 63, 65, 88
Volhynia (Wojciech Smarzowski film) 46–7
Volker, Kurt 95
Von Hagen, Mark 2
Vynnychenko, Volodymyr 24
Vyšné Nemecké (formerly Oberdeutschdorf) 1
Vyzhnytsia 110

Wanner, Catherine 17n9
Warsaw Pact 95
'West Ukrainian People's Republic' (ZUNR) 24, 25

Westminster Foundation 94
White, Hayden 3, 7n5
Whitlock, Greg 67n14
Wilkins, Sophie 39n4
The Will to Power (Gast, P. and Förster-Nietzsche, E.) 61
Wilson, Andrew 7n7
Winter War (1939–1940) 91
With Fire and Sword (Sienkiewicz, H.) 43
Woldan, Alois 39n5
Wolff, Andrew T. 98n10
Wolowyna, Oleh 66–7n4
A Woman in Berlin (anonymous diary, 2003) 59
World Bank 78
World Press Freedom Index (2019) 101
World Trade Organization (WTO) 80

Yalovy, Mykhailo 26
Yalta 110–11; Conference at (1945) 95
Yandex 101
Yanukovych, Viktor 3–4, 13, 16, 35, 62, 97, 102; authoritarianism of 5; economic conditions and 79, 80, 81, 82; election of, street protests against 28; European Union (EU) and 85, 90, 91; federal structure for Ukraine, promotion of 55; Holodomor issue under presidency of 59; language policy of 11; legitimacy of, loss of basis for 52; Putin and, relationship between 70
Yatsenyuk, Arseniy 32, 62, 82, 83–4
Yelensky, Viktor 17n9
Yesmukhanova, Yulia 56n11
Yohansen, Maik 26
Yushchenko, Viktor 14, 15, 29, 30, 59, 102; economic conditions and 78, 81, 82; historical events, policies concerning 62; Holodomor issue and 60; NATO membership, priority for 69, 96; United States, promotion of alliance with 94

Zakharchenko, Alexander 73
Zaleski, Józef Bohdan 42–3
Zaporizhia 111; language spoken in 12; LOT flights to 41
Zelensky, Volodymyr 52, 82, 102–3
Zurabov, Mikhail 73

For Product Safety Concerns and Information please contact our EU representative GPSR@taylorandfrancis.com
Taylor & Francis Verlag GmbH, Kaufingerstraße 24, 80331 München, Germany

www.ingramcontent.com/pod-product-compliance
Lightning Source LLC
Chambersburg PA
CBHW070556170426
43201CB00012B/1860